TECHNOLOGY AND SOCIETY

TECHNOLOGY AND SOCIETY

Advisory Editor
DANIEL J. BOORSTIN, author of
The Americans and Director of
The National Museum of History
and Technology, Smithsonian Institution

WHEREVER MEN TRADE

The Romance of the Cash Register

By

ISAAC F. MARCOSSON

ARNO PRESS

A NEW YORK TIMES COMPANY

New York • 1972

Reprint Edition 1972 by Arno Press Inc.

Reprinted from a copy in The University of
Illinois Library

Technology and Society
ISBN for complete set: 0-405-04680-4
See last pages of this volume for titles.

Manufactured in the United States of America

———————

Library of Congress Cataloging in Publication Data

Marcosson, Isaac Frederick, 1876-1961.
    Wherever men trade.

    (Technology and society)
    Reprint of the 1945 ed.
    1. Cash registers. 2. Patterson, John Henry, 1844-
1922. 3. National Cash Register Company, Dayton.
I. Title. II. Series.
HF5531.M3 1972   338.4'7'6814   72-5062
ISBN 0-405-04713-4

WHEREVER MEN TRADE

John H. Patterson

WHEREVER MEN TRADE

The Romance of the Cash Register

By

ISAAC F. MARCOSSON

With Illustrations

New York

Dodd, Mead & Company

1945

TO

THE MEMORY OF
JOHN H. PATTERSON

Whose vision and venture made
The National Cash Register
Company Possible

FOREWORD

FOR six decades The National Cash Register
Company has maintained the tradition of its
founder. This tradition was reared on increased efficiency and service for retail business.
It launched the era of cash register economy which
expanded to the epoch of larger business machine
utility. Protection for the merchant has been paral-
leled by mechanized systems for industry and banking. The applications of NCR products now
influence the operation of nearly every aspect of
commercial activity.

Today the world faces a stupendous task of reconversion—the transformation of the proverbial
sword into a plowshare. In the fiery furnace of
war new concepts of production have been forged
that will affect the output of the future. Just as industry went to war "full speed ahead" so will it go
to peace with enhanced knowledge and increased
facility. The corporation and the community together will contribute anew to the lifting of the
standard of life and labor.

In the industrial laboratory lie the formulae for
the shape of mechanized things to come. The

still unplumbed possibilities await translation into
new devices to serve the hand and brain of mankind. In this drama of development The National
Cash Register Company will play its full part,
capitalizing the new tools of industry wrought by
research. The cash register will become more and
more an accounting machine and the accounting
machine will expand to wider applications. As in
the past, we will progress through change.

We count ourselves fortunate in being able to secure Mr. Marcosson as historian for the Company.
His long friendship with John H. Patterson, his
knowledge of the business extending over more than
thirty years, and his rich equipment as international
economic observer place him in an unusual position
to present the Cash Register story.

E. A. DEEDS

October, 1945.

CONTENTS

WHEREVER MEN TRADE

CHAPTER I

A Machine Is Born

A MAN of small physical stature but stoked with dynamic energy was operating a retail coal business in Dayton and a general store in the Ohio coal field back in the eighties. The store was losing money through the peculations of clerks. One day the man heard of a machine that recorded retail sales. Without waiting to investigate it he telegraphed for three of them. The use of the machines in the store converted loss into profit.

The man was John H. Patterson; the machine was the cash register. Within a few years he acquired the business that produced the registers. The product was practically unknown; the demand for it had to be created. Capitalizing his genius for organization and dramatizing his perception of selling, Patterson made the world his market and his cash register an indispensable aid to business.

The approach to the cash register down the long corridor of the years discloses a little known but picturesque chapter in the evolution of the human race. It is the story of accounting through the ages. From the beginning of time man has coveted possessions.

1

Linked with the process of acquiring them was the problem of counting them. Primitive peoples had their methods of recording their belongings, whether wives or weapons, no less primitive than their way of life.

Counting is as old as civilization itself. In prehistoric times man was able to differentiate between a large number and a smaller one and to appreciate the difference between them. Hence evolved the "number sense." The first method of counting was with the fingers which formed the earliest of calculating machines. Pebbles were also employed as numerals. Our word "calculate" is derived from the Latin *"calculi"* which means "to count with pebbles." Coincident with the finger and pebble era was the use of knotted fibers for counting.

The ancient Babylonians, master traders of their period, provided a durable system of recording the results of their counting which was done with fingers, pebbles, or markings on a dust-board. They registered contracts, sales, customs duties, bonds, and wrote receipts on tablets of clay which were baked in the sun. The quality of the clay and the climatic conditions under which it was produced, rendered these records impervious to time. Records imprinted on clay tablets thousands of years before the dawn of Christianity are in good condition today.

Recording made a further advance under the old Egyptians, Romans, and Greeks who wrote on papyrus for the registration of financial transactions. The

wealthy class only could indulge in this luxury. Poor
people were obliged to scratch their accounts on frag-
ments of pottery which was highly perishable.

In England the Domesday Book, which registered
all taxable estates, was perhaps the fore-runner of
permanent accounting in the kingdom. Tangible
accounting began later with a system unique in the
history of recorded figures. The medium was the so-
called Tally Sticks. They were splints of elm wood
with notches cut in them. Each notch represented a
certain sum paid. These sticks resembled the crude
calendar kept by Robinson Crusoe on his desert island. The Tally Sticks were introduced in the Court
of the Exchequer during the Middle Ages mainly to
record the payment of taxes. When the honest yeo-
man paid his tithe the amount was cut on the Tally
Stick which was then split into two sections. The
Exchequer kept one while the taxpayer retained the
other which acted as a crude form of receipt.

Although England was cluttered with accountants, bookkeepers, and actuaries with pens, paper,
slates, and ink in wide use, the authorities clung to
this primitive reckoning until 1826. A vast quantity
of the sticks had accumulated. It was suggested that
all this financial timber be given to the poor for
firewood. However, one obstreperous parliamen-
tarian objected and it was decided to burn the wood
in a stove in the House of Lords. The flames got
out of hand, set fire to the panelling, with the re-

sult that the House of Parliament burned to the ground.

While some primitive peoples still exercised their fingers or used pebbles to count their belongings, the first known mechanical calculating contrivance helped to dispel arithmetical headaches in various parts of the world. It was the abacus which is almost as an old as history. Until the beginning of the Christian era it was the only actual counting instrument that mankind possessed. The abacus was probably invented by the Semitic races and is said to have been used in China as long ago as 2637 B.C.

The original abacus was a device for tracing numerals on a dust-covered board. Subsequently the board was covered with wax and became the forerunner of the modern slate.

A different type of abacus developed from man's usage of pebbles or beads for numbers. Originally he discarded them when he finished his calculation. This led to the counting frame. At first this form of abacus was a series of grooves on a flat surface, the beads or pebbles being placed in the grooves. Later it became a set of upright sticks on which pierced stones, shells, or beads could be strung. Eventually the closed frame superseded the earlier type. Among the first to employ this form of abacus were the peoples living on the shores of the Mediterranean.

The abacus was also adopted in very early times in India whence it spread along the trade and cultural routes of the world. When the Spanish Conquistadors came to Mexico and Peru they found a form of abacus in use among the Aztecs and the Incas. It is still largely employed in India, China, and Japan. The Japanese are particularly expert in its use.

More than one royal hand has fingered the beads of the abacus. Among the loot taken by the Communists when they seized the Czar's summer palace just outside the one-time St. Petersburg was an abacus used by the last of the Czarinas. It was exquisitely wrought of silver with topaz and crystal beads, and represented the handiwork of Karl Faberge, the Court Jeweller.

The abacus, however, was merely a mile-post on the long journey toward a machine capable of performing arithmetical operations. Perhaps the pioneer mechanism designed to facilitate calculation was the so-called Rods of Napier, produced by Lord Napier, inventor of logarithms, who lived in the 16th and 17th centuries. It was an impractical and cumbersome series of devices, mainly rods and cells, which could be applied only to multiplication.

The real ancestor of the modern calculating machine was an apparatus devised by Blaise Pascal, a distinguished figure in 17th century French scientific and literary circles. Pascal, whose father was a judge, asked his son to help him with his accounts. Seeking to eliminate the monotony of mental calculation, he built a machine crude in construction but sound in principle, which added figures and produced a total. It was demonstrated before the Court of Louis XIV in 1642.

Certain of man's proclivities, particularly his aversion to unnecessary labor, are immemorial. The calculating boards of the ancients, the abacus and her daughters, the Rods of Napier, and Pascal's contrivance, all involved a degree of mental effort. Man yearned for some kind of accounting machine that would be automatic and therefore spare him mental exertion. This is why so many investigators of the 17th and 18th centuries concentrated on a counting machine that would be self-operating.

It was not until 1820 that Charles Xavier Thomas, a Frenchman, gave the world the first commercially successful calculating machine which performed the four operations of addition, subtraction, division, and multiplication. This was the basis of all subsequent calculating machines. It did not print results but merely tabulated them.

Sixty years after Thomas perfected his mechanism William Seward Burroughs contributed the first adding machine. Now for the first time there existed a machine that not only added items but also printed the list of these items and the total as well. The comptometer, invented by Dorr E. Felt, was a further step in the march of mechanical counting. The calculating machine, the adding machine, and the comptometer began to play a considerable part in relieving business, especially banking, of time-consuming and irksome mental mathematical effort. Meanwhile fare boxes for street cars with counters and an indicator to register fares paid; simple forms of voting machines; meters for gas and water; and billiard room registers for keeping scores of games had come into use, making a definite contribution to accurate accounting as well as labor saving. The era of mechanical calculation which was to fit into the larger era of mechanization, whether for war or peace, had begun.

The more or less simple machines that have been enumerated met only part of a great need. They lacked the protective feature so essential to the conduct of retail business where money is handled. The open cash drawer, save for the merchant's pocket, was the sole receptacle for cash paid by a customer in a store. Alarm bells on cash drawers failed to safeguard receipts. The tradesman was at the mercy of the unscrupulous clerk who could pilfer the till at will.

It remained for James Ritty, an obscure Dayton cafe owner, in collaboration with his brother John, to invent a machine that for the first time offered protection for the retail merchant. By putting indicators, that is, tablets registering the amount of a sale, in the machine he made it possible for the customer to check or audit the amount of his purchase. Such was the chief function of the pioneer cash register, destined to revolutionize the financial aspect of retail merchandising the world over.

The period that witnessed the birth of the cash register was rich in American mechanical advance. Peaceful conquest of the continent was complete. The Civil War sword had become a plowshare that was furrowing a new empire of agricultural production. The covered wagon was an heroic memory. During the first half of the nineteenth century, power-driven American machines had changed the face of the industrial map. We had ceased to be a reservoir of raw materials for the factories of Europe and had struck the creative stride destined to give us a far-flung production prestige. The Epoch of Oil had opened; the dawn of the Age of Steel was breaking. East and West were linked in a network of communications. The significant movement from farm to factory had begun. By the close of the War between the States more than one-third of our population supported itself wholly or in part by the manufacturing industry. The industrial revolution was in full swing.

Society and business demanded new aids to comfort and convenience. The vast processes of change that had initiated the urban movement stimulated the inventive mind and American ingenuity met the challenge. The telephone, the typewriter, the phonograph, and the incandescent light preceded the cash register. Selden's first patent for the gasoline carriage was almost coincident. The fountain pen, the arc lamp, and the first electric street car lurked around the corner. Machines were supplanting muscle; economy was being transformed. The tools of American life became more practical, accessible, and efficient.

Out of this era of hacks, gaslight, bustles, Prince Albert coats and wooden Indians emerged the cash register. Like the telephone, the telegraph, and the automobile it was fated for the clash of bitter patent war and endured a kindred ordeal of opposition and worse. Yet it developed into a necessity for business upon which today the sun never sets. The story of its march from obscure beginning to an indispensable aid to merchandising is a romance of American industrial achievement.

When Ritty invented the cash register in 1878 he fitted into what might be termed the pattern of the inventor. As various historians of invention have pointed out, many of the men who have contributed notably to mechanical progress came not from within, but from without, industry. Cartwright, who invented the power loom, was poet and clergyman. Whitney, the cotton gin inventor, was a teacher who never had the slightest connection with cotton production. Howe and Singer, pioneers of the sewing machine, probably did not see the inside of a clothing factory until long after their patents were in use. Westinghouse was not a railway employee yet he devised the air brake. Fulton of steamboat fame and Morse, father of telegraph, were artists. Bell was a teacher of the deaf long before he transformed communication with the telephone. Thus it came about that James Ritty took his humble place in this gallery of giants of invention. He was a cafe owner whose primary purpose in creating the first cash register was to protect the cash receipts in his business.

James Ritty was one of five brothers. Their father, Leger Ritty, emigrated from Alsace Lorraine and settled in Dayton, Ohio. Leger Ritty was a dispenser of drugs made of herbs. He established an office in the southwestern section of Dayton and built up a considerable practice. During a cholera epidemic "Dr." Ritty, as he was known, compounded remedies that helped to combat the disease.

Three of the Ritty brothers Sebastin, John and James were of an inventive turn of mind. Sebastin took out a number of patents on farm implements. John, ultimately to be associated with James in the invention of the cash register, was a mechanic by trade and carried on the inventive tradition of the family. Among other things, he patented several machines for the hulling of green corn and set up a canning factory in which they were used. He also operated a restaurant and cafe. There is a story, still current in Dayton, that his ingenuity was revealed in a unique device. He piped water to all the tables in his restaurant and used the water power to operate motors which rotated palm leaf fans for the comfort of his patrons in hot weather.

Hence James Ritty, who was the youngest of the brothers, grew up in an atmosphere that encouraged invention. His association with invention, however, was purely accidental. Although trained as a mechanic he forsook work with his hands and opened a cafe variously known as "No. 10" and "The Empire" in a three-story building at 10 South Main Street in Dayton. This location was destined to be historic in the annals of business. Here, in a small room on the second floor, the cash register was born.

Progressive and intelligent, James Ritty was a "good mixer" and a man about town. Of medium height, stocky build, with alert eyes and a drooping moustache, he was invariably well turned out. He sported a silk hat in and out of his cafe. Ritty had the qualities essential to the successful conduct of a saloon, and he made the most of them. Although his business flourished he lost money. The reason was not obscure. Like every other retail establishment of the day that handled money over the counter, in his case it was over the bar, the only receptable for receipts, save the pocket of the proprietor, was a cash drawer. It could be easily opened with the result that bartenders were able to hold out as much cash as they desired. The open cash drawer was an ever-present temptation to the weak-willed. A constant turnover of bartenders brought Ritty no relief.

Ritty brooded so much over the peculations in his business that he suffered a breakdown and was obliged to take a vacation trip to Europe. His traveling companion was Captain Bogardus, a famous expert shot, who was to give exhibitions of his markmanship abroad. Now developed one of those incidents that chart the course of invention. Having been trained as a mechanic Ritty became interested in the machinery of the ship. An agreeable and companionable fellow, he made friends with the Chief Engineer on the eastbound voyage. Soon he had the run of the engine room.

One day he stood fascinated before the automatic mechanism that recorded the revolutions of the ship's propeller shaft. With his thoughts still fixed on the losses in his cafe and how to circumvent them, he had an inspiration. To himself he said:

"If the movements of a ship's propeller can be recorded there is no reason why the movements of sales in a store cannot be recorded. There is a great field for a machine that can do this work."

From that inspired moment, amid the din and clash of a ship's engine room, the idea of the cash register began to take shape in Ritty's mind. He became so obsessed with the thought that he cut short his stay in Europe and returned to Dayton. He confided the idea to his brother John. Together they began to work on a machine that was to make mechanical history. Born as a crude mechanism in the dawn of mechanization, the principles of the cash register were as logical in conception and as unerring in purpose as the telephone and the automobile.

The first model had two rows of keys across the lower front of the machine. Pressed down, each key represented the individual amount of money to be recorded. The sales were registered on a face resembling the face of a wall clock or a steam gauge. There was no cash drawer in this earliest effort. Although incomplete in many details, the machine was the first outpost in the long line of protection that the cash register was to give to the retail merchant in the years to come.

The Rittys then made a second machine resembling the first in all details with one exception. Instead of adding disks the brothers designed a series of adding wheels mounted in the back of the machine. This machine was patented November 4, 1879. It was the first United States patent ever issued for a cash register. Neither of these two models was put on the market.

Apparently dissatisfied with their dial models, the Rittys now began a new line of development. Instead of the dial type of indication they substituted a tablet form which is still used on many types of cash registers. The tablet indicators were small plates bearing the same money values imprinted on the top of the keys, and were connected with the indicators by vertical sliding rods. As a key was depressed the indicator rod, resting on the key, was elevated until the indicator showed through a glass-covered opening in the upper part of the machine.

This was an important advance because the exact amount of the sale was revealed to both clerk and customer. The indicator was one of the early fundamental features of the cash register which has continued in use to the present day. From the start it meant increased protection for the merchant because it shed the light of publicity on every transaction. There was still no cash drawer in the third machine which the inventors called "Ritty's Incorruptible Cashier." This type was not sold to the public.

The next machine came to be known as the "detail adder" or paper roll machine. James Ritty mounted a wide paper roll horizontally above and across the keys inside the machine. Each key carried a sharp pin. When the key was depressed, its pin pricked a hole in the roll of paper just above the key. At the same time the paper roll would be advanced, or fed, one step. The result was that at the end of the day's business the proprietor could remove the roll of paper, unroll the portion representing the day's sales, and count the holes in each column. If there were ten holes in the five cent column, he simply multiplied ten by five which told him that he had done a fifty cent business in five cent sales. He could repeat the counting of holes in each of the other columns of holes and then add them all up to get the grand total of sales for the day. Thus the register not only told the owner the exact amount of the day's business but also the total done in each price range.

The paper roll machine marked an epoch in the progress of the cash register. It was the first to be put on sale, heralding an output and an expansion that became the marvel of the machine age. More important was the fact that it was this model which came to the attention of John H. Patterson who bought three of the machines and installed them in his general store at Coalton, Ohio. These registers, sold to Patterson, were the first to be installed in a mercantile establishment. All previous sales had been made to bar and cafe owners.

Fate must have been lurking about when the Patterson transaction was consummated. Before very long Patterson was to become the pioneer of cash register production and to make his name synonymous with its development and distribution.

James Ritty launched the cash register business under the name of "James Ritty's New Cash Register and Indicator," in a little room over his cafe at 10 South Main Street. Apparently he did some advertising because registers were shipped to different parts of the country. The most distant order was from Duluth, Minnesota.

By October 1881 the infant cash register industry was beginning to emerge from its swaddling clothes. James Ritty needed more room so he moved to larger quarters. Here John Ritty was foreman. The factory force numbered ten men. Since the first machines that appeared on the market were largely constructed of wood, most of the employees were carpenters and cabinet makers, a trade which James Ritty had followed in previous years.

James Ritty encountered hard sledding in his efforts to build up the cash register business. He still conducted the cafe which demanded the major part

of his time. In later years he confessed that he
"simply could not direct the cash register business."
Commenting on his failure he once said:

"If any one other than John H. Patterson had
gotten the business, the cash register industry would
never have been a success." Events prior to 1885
bore out this statement.

Following nearly two years of struggle, James
and John Ritty sold their entire cash register business, including patents, to Jacob H. Eckert for
$1,000. Eckert had been a salesman for a Cincinnati
china and glassware firm which brought him into
frequent contact with cafe and restaurant operators
who were among the first to purchase cash registers.
Eckert infused new life into the business. Within a
week he moved the factory. In the new quarters
began a more intensive manufacture of three sizes
of the paper roll machine.

Meanwhile various important improvements were
made in the register. They were the inventions of
John Birch, a machinist and brother-in-law of
Eckert. These improvements shaped the future
course of the machine because they embodied basic
features of permanent value.

When Eckert purchased the cash register business
none of the machines was equipped with a drawer.
One of the first innovations was the introduction by
Birch of a drawer and a bell that rang when the key
was depressed and the drawer opened. This bell
sounded the note of future success. The time would

come when, like the historic Revolutionary shot fired at Lexington, it would be heard around the world.

Eckert's introduction of the cash drawer and bell was the final link in the combination of indication, adding mechanism, and cash drawer which compelled the clerk to go to the register and ring up a sale in order to have access to the drawer. It forced him to deposit the money received and to pay out the change. Here, at last, was real protection. The indicator showed the customer the amount registered on the sale. The proprietor was assured that the amount registered was placed in the cash drawer, and that the proper record would be made by the adding mechanism. Publicity joined with protection in safeguarding receipts. Another major improvement was the substitution of a series of wheels for the paper roll. The purpose of the wheels was to keep a record of the number of times each key was operated. It eliminated the necessity of counting holes as obtained in the paper roll machine.

This advance was the joint work of James Ritty and Birch and was covered by a patent assigned to Eckert when he bought the business in 1881. The patent formed the basis of a large part of the early litigation between the subsequent National Cash Register Company and the large number of competitors who sprang up all over the country.

Up to 1881 the Rittys had operated as a partnership under the name of The National Cash Register Company. This was the first use of the name which was to become famous under John H. Patterson. By 1882 Eckert realized that he could not swing the cash register business on his own. Early in 1882, in conjunction with William Kiefaber, Gustavus W. and William Sander, and Benjamin W. Early who had become associates, he organized The National Manufacturing Company with a capital stock of $10,000 divided into 200 shares of $50 par value each. Later on the capital was increased to $15,000. There were 300 shares of $50 par value each. Birch was one of the incorporators. The company acquired all the Ritty-Birch patents from Eckert who owned the controlling interest and was represented on the Board of Directors by his wife. The National Manufacturing Company continued to make cash registers until the fall of 1883 when it changed its quarters to the Callahan Power Building in an alley between Second and Third Streets, east of Main.

The year 1883 was historic in the history of the cash register because it witnessed the entry of John H. Patterson into the business. His was a modest participation at first, but it opened the way for what became a dominant part. In May he appeared on the books of the company as the owner of 25 shares. Soon after he became a member of the Board and was later elected Secretary. This was his first official connection with the company. At the annual meeting held in January 1884 it was disclosed that he held only 20 shares. His brother Frank, later a close associate in the development of the business, who had

also acquired some of the stock, now owned no shares
at all. Early in 1884 John H. retired as a director.
The Patterson hiatus, however, was brief.

Since John H. Patterson was on the verge of control of the company it may be well, at this point, to
get his background which will provide the approach
to the crowded and fruitful years that lay ahead for
him. His ancestry helped to shape his career and
give him the heritage of courage and aggressiveness
which were among his dominant qualities. He
sprang from sturdy Revolutionary stock. His grand-
father, Colonel Robert Patterson, who fought under
George Washington, founded Lexington, Kentucky,
and was also one of the founders of Cincinnati. He
ultimately settled on what came to be known as Rubicon Farm just south of Dayton. His youngest son
Jefferson, one of ten children, was the father of John
H., who was born December 13th, 1844 on the original homestead in Dayton. Here he spent his boyhood serving a hardy apprenticeship in work. Like
many other Americans who rose to distinction he
obtained his early education in a little red school
house.

After graduating from Central High School in
Dayton he entered Miami University at Oxford,
Ohio. Since three of his brothers were serving in the
Federal Army, John was forced to interrupt his
studies and return to the farm to help his mother.
When Lincoln issued his call for volunteers to serve
100 days John enlisted. After his honorable dis-

charge he became a student at Dartmouth College, graduating in the class of 1867.

Patterson found this his college education apparently fitted him for everything but a job. After a brief experience as school teacher he got the position of toll-collector on the Miami and Erie Canal. His salary was $800 a year but he had to spend $300 for office rent and incidentals. He was on duty twenty-four hours a day because boats came through at all times. He lived in a small room which was also his office.

After a few months he realized that his net yearly income of $500 was inadequate so he decided to go into the coal business on the side. He hung up a sign proclaiming "Coal and Wood" outside his office. When he received an order he bought coal from a dealer and hired some one to deliver it. His day book was a slate. When an account was settled he wiped it off. In this crude way the future magnate of the cash register began his commercial career.

Patterson had big ideas even when he had a little business. He heard that a coal dealer located nearby wanted to sell out. He borrowed $250 from a local bank and bought the business. The assets were a tumble-down coal yard, a pair of scales, two carts, some coal, lime, cement and wood, and two blind horses. John took his brother Stephen into partnership and opened up shop as S. J. Patterson & Co. By 1876 the firm was doing so well that John H. gave up his job as toll-collector.

From the start John H. was meticulous in his dealings with customers. He needed no Marguery of Paris to tell him that "the customer is always right." He sold the best coal, used spirited horses to draw his brightly painted carts, and advertised liberally. In that early day he revealed the basis of the sound business procedure upon which a world-wide enterprise was later to be reared. One detail will illustrate.

Some of Patterson's customers disputed the quantity of coal for which they were charged and the amounts they were required to pay. Since every complaint was a personal matter Patterson devised a system of receipt tickets for both coal and cash. I dwell on this episode because it was John H. Patterson who first put the receipt on a cash register thus introducing a notable step in its development. The receipt is a commonplace today but when Patterson first used it in his retail coal business it was a distinct novelty.

Patterson's determination to create good will as well as good business led him into unconventional procedure. He had obtained the agency for Jackson County coal. It was good coal but sometimes it had to be coaxed before it caught fire. It followed that on occasion Patterson had complaints about it.

At the root of his business creed was education which always meant training. He later applied it to every detail of his cash register production and selling. In that early day he demonstrated it with his customers. Although co-head of the coal firm he visited customers' homes, went into kitchens and showed cooks and housewives how to get the fire started. There were no caste lines in his teaching code. He went from the residences of the socially elect to tenements. Often he would turn up in a kitchen almost before the household was astir.

John H. Patterson's scrupulous attention to details and his liberal expenditures for advertising irked Stephen who, being older, believed in more conservative methods. In consequence, the partnership was dissolved in 1879, Stephen buying out John's interest. With his youngest brother Frank J., John now organized the new coal firm of Patterson & Company. The first period of expansion in John's business life began.

Although handicapped by lack of capital John began to widen the firm's activities. The coal they sold came from the Coalton and Wellston fields by a roundabout way which increased the freight overhead. John H. started a movement which led to the building of a direct line—the Dayton & South eastern—from the mines to Dayton. The Patterson brothers now decided to mine their own coal so they leased mines at Coalton and Wellston. John H. borrowed $15,000 and had 52 coal cars built for the firm's use. They bore the inscription "Patterson & Co." in large vivid letters. John H. always believed in business publicity. The firm flourished. By this time John H. and Frank were operating three coal mines, a chain of retail yards, and a general store at Coalton, Ohio.

While operating the store at Coalton John H. Patterson had his first actual contact with the cash register. He had practically no competition, no bad debts; paid cash for all he bought, and did a big business, that is big, for the locality. At the end of two years he had lost $3,000. He suffered from the same malady that had played havoc with James Ritty's profits. His clerks, with an open cash drawer constantly conjuring up temptation, purloined part of the daily receipts.

One day he heard of a Dayton-made machine that registered sales. Without inquiring the price he telegraphed for three of them. They were the original paper roll machines. Within six months the store showed a profit of several thousand dollars. The cash registers had turned the trick for there was no more pilfering. Patterson was so impressed with the results that he ordered two registers for his retail coal business in Dayton.

In 1881 John H. Patterson embarked for the first and only time in his life in a business that he did not control. A group of Boston capitalists tied up a network of narrow gauge railroads in Ohio and Indiana, including the Dayton and South Eastern, into a single system. Then they decided to go into the coal business. John H. and Frank Patterson had become known as the most alert and progressive operators in the Jackson County field. The eastern financiers en-

gaged them to acquire coal mines which were sold to
a corporation, The Southern Ohio Coal and Iron
Company, which they formed to operate the properties. The Pattersons took over the management of
the mines and the sale of the product receiving an
allocation of stock and bonds for their services. They
continued their retail coal business in Dayton, after
selling their own mines and leasing their equipment
to the corporation.

The association with the Southern Ohio Coal and
Iron Company was not altogether happy. John H.
Patterson was a minority stockholder. Being wilful
and impatient, he chafed under the restraint that
this imposed. He was born to control and he had no
control over the properties he managed. Frank, who
was much less temperamental, took things in his
stride.

John H.'s dissatisfaction with the situation led to
two events. One was the retirement of the brothers
from association with The Southern Ohio Coal and
Iron Company. The other was the sale of their coal
business in Dayton. For the first time since he established himself in the little toll-keeper's office on the
Miami and Erie Canal John was free to do as he
pleased.

A year prior to their retirement from all branches
of the coal business John H. and Frank had made
their initial investment in The National Manufacturing Company with the purchase of 50 shares. John
H. was the instigator because he had a strong con-

viction, based on his experience with cash registers both at Coalton and Dayton, that the machine had a future. The cash register business, however, was not getting anywhere. The annual statement of the company, issued early in 1884, showed a loss. This discouraged Frank to such an extent that he disposed of all of his shares. John H. could only get rid of five. This explains how it happened that he appeared on the books of the company as owner of 20 shares at the annual meeting held in January 1884. His retirement as a director followed.

It was impossible for a man of John H. Patterson's temperament to remain idle. As he cast about for an activity to engage his energy his thoughts reverted to those rigorous boyhood days on the Rubicon Farm. He was torn between farming and manufacturing. For the moment some occupation on the land seemed to win out. In his impulsive way he said to Frank:

"We should get into a business with limitless possibilities. Nearly everybody eats meat. Let us buy a ranch and raise cattle."

When Patterson spoke of "limitless possibilities" he revealed the extent of the vision that was to lead him to the industrial heights. Always impatient of petty details, he saw life and work in a large way.

Frank was agreeable to the cattle-raising suggestion. In May 1884 the brothers set forth for the West which still beckoned to the seeker of business and other adventure. For four months they ranged through half a dozen States from Missouri to California. Late in September they paused at the Antlers Hotel in Colorado Springs to take stock of their travels, and to decide which one of three ranches, on which they had options, to buy.

As is the case with most successful men John H. Patterson was always athirst for information. An inveterate cross-examiner, he invariably pumped people dry. He learned from everybody he questioned whether bootblack or banker.

While sitting in the lobby of The Antlers one evening he engaged in conversation with a New England merchant. When he discovered that the man expected to remain on holiday for two months he asked:

"How can you afford to leave your business so long?"

"That is not difficult," replied the man. "I have a capable manager and I own a cash register made in Dayton. Every day my manager sends me a statement together with the punched roll from the machine. I can keep a perfect check on my business."

John H. was deeply impressed. The merchant's experience was identical with his own in the retail coal business and the general store at Coalton. He said to Frank:

"What was good for our stores and for this man's business in New England is good for every store in the world. The cash register business can be developed into one of the great industries of America."

With this pregnant observation the cattle ranch

idea, happily for American business, went glimmering. On the following day the brothers started back to Dayton, determined to purchase control of The National Manufacturing Company.

John H. Patterson was the type of man around whom legends cluster. It follows that there is one concerning his purchase of the cash register business. Variations on the original tale exist. The facts, sifted out from the romance which envelops the story, are these:

On the evening of the day the Pattersons arrived in Dayton—it was now late in October—they had a long talk with George L. Phillips, President of The National Manufacturing Company, who owned the controlling interest. Phillips was a well-known Dayton capitalist who organized the first telephone exchange in the city. John H. agreed to buy the Phillips stock for $6500. After the deal had been closed, save for the actual payment, the brothers went over to the Dayton Club where they spoke enthusiastically about the transaction. What they did not know was that The National Manufacturing Company had become something of a jest in town. It had lost money steadily and was looked upon as a failure. It followed that when the Pattersons spoke so glowingly about their purchase of control they were met with jokes and even jeers.

The banter at the club depressed and discouraged John H. He went home that night determined to cancel the deal with Phillips the first thing next

morning. Just why he got cold feet on the product
to which he subsequently dedicated himself is
inexplicable. John H. Patterson, however, was a ca-
pricious person. It was difficult at times to understand what motivated certain of his actions.

When Patterson sought to retire from the deal he
was thwarted. Phillips insisted that the strict letter
of the arrangement be carried out. Patterson then
offered him $2,000 for a release from his obligation.
Phillips remained adamant. To Patterson he is reported to have said:

"You have purchased the stock. If you had paid
for it and I had turned it over to you, I would not
have it back as a gift."

"Very well," replied Patterson. "I am going into
the cash register business and I will make a success
of it. You will be sorry later on."

Every outstanding industry sets up mile-posts of
its progress. So it was with cash register production
which now entered upon the first phase of what became a momentous advance. The time had arrived
when the chief protagonist in the drama of its development stepped on the scene. That protagonist
was John H. Patterson.

Soon after he acquired control Patterson changed
the corporate name of the company back to that of
The National Cash Register Company. At the stockholders' meeting held on January 5, 1885 he was revealed as the owner of 227 shares out of a total of
300. Frank Patterson had one share. The following

year the capital stock was increased to $100,000, divided into 2,000 shares of $50 par value each. Meanwhile John H. had acquired the shares of Charles Whelan and William Sander, the only other stockholders, thus establishing complete Patterson control of the business. It was to remain a family affair until after the death of John H. Patterson in 1922.

The hesitancy in the deal with Phillips was obviously a passing phase with Patterson. Once committed to the cash register it became the passion of his life, charged with the fire and fervor of a crusade.

CHAPTER II

"Life Begins at Forty"

WHEN John H. Patterson assumed control of the National Cash Register Company in 1884 he was forty years old. At a time when most men were well launched on their life's work he was embarking on a new vocation. Patterson personified all that the word "contradiction" implies. He knew little or nothing about mechanics yet he successfully developed a machine that helped to revolutionize retail business. Although not a salesman, as such, he created a technique of selling that has stood the test of time.

Let us visualize Patterson as he stood on the threshold of his industrial career. Almost undersized, he was wiry, with gray eyes, florid complexion, sandy hair, and bristling moustache. He was, as someone put it, "a little man with a dynamo inside." Dominated by a ruthless will, and driven by a restless energy, he was both doer and dreamer. Like the character in the Kipling poem he could "meet with Triumph and Disaster" and "treat these two impostors just the same." Divorced from his eccentricities he stood revealed as a great leader and teacher of

men. He made men as well as machines. He had a
keen appreciation of showmanship but he did not
dramatize himself. He dramatized his product.
Such was the type of man who now applied himself
to the difficult task of placing practically an unknown
machine on the market.

Like many other industrial enterprises that expanded to commanding proportions, The National
Cash Register Company started in humble circumstances. Patterson's first factory on the second floor
of the Callahan Power Building was forty feet wide
and eighty feet long. This included work and office
space. Thirteen people were on the pay-roll. The
equipment consisted of a small punch press, one large
lathe, one milling machine, two bench lathes, a printing press, two drill presses, a forge and some vises,
and equipment for printing indicators. The output
was four or five registers a week. The workmen sat
on boxes for there were no stools.

On the third morning after Patterson took over
direction of the business the workmen discovered that
the boxes were gone. They stood around grumbling
when he entered the work room. Seeing the glum
faces Patterson asked:

"Well, boys, what is wrong?"

"Where are our boxes?" demanded the foreman.

"Don't worry," responded Patterson. "You will
have stools before the day is over." By nightfall the
stools had been installed.

From the start John H. was absorbed in the planning, selling, and advertising ends while Frank took over factory management. John was volatile and highstrung; Frank steady and conservative, ever the wise counsellor and balance wheel of the business. Although more or less obscured by the spectacular methods of his brother, Frank was a definite force in the development of the business until his death in 1901. The career of the two Pattersons was not unlike that of the Wright brothers of airplane fame. In each instance success evolved from close teamwork.

The Patterson stock in trade in those precarious mid-eighties was exactly two types of register. One was the paper roll machine; the other the wheel detail adder. When The National Cash Register Company had rounded out sixty years of progress in 1944 those two early registers had grown to a line of more than 600 styles and sizes including accounting machines which represented a notable later development. These machines meet the needs of three hundred and fifty different businesses from soda fountains and cafeterias by way of hotels and department stores to banks and industries. John H. Patterson would be stirred with pride and satisfaction if he could behold the vista of expansion that stretches from his pioneering day.

The cash register encountered the opposition that useful innovation has invariably evoked. The time is within living memory when the drivers of the first automobiles were greeted with the admonition, "Get a horse!"; when the telephone was regarded as a fad; when Shank's mare was preferable to the first electric street cars; when people dismissed the typewriter with the remark: "Why spend $125 for a machine to do the work of a one cent pen?" Cash registers had a more difficult path to follow than these products. To prejudice against novelty was the added obstacle of what in present day parlance would be called a racket. It was the practice of pilfering cash drawers in retail establishments

The situation that confronted John H. Patterson took full toll of his resource. He was obliged to accomplish three purposes. One was to allay the resentment against "a new fangled machine." Second was to demonstrate the economy, efficiency, and service of the cash register. Third was the confutation of the dishonest clerk entrenched behind years of uninterrupted graft. In short, Patterson had to create a demand for a product where no demand existed. Thus began what the history of salesmanship in America records as "creative selling."

Patterson's first selling force numbered five men who were called upon to introduce a product that apparently no one wanted. Wherever they sought to sell they met antagonism, even hostility. Pilfering clerks who feared the end of their "easy money" went so far as to organize groups to combat what they dubbed a "thief catcher." The sales agents were often forced to carry catalogues in their umbrellas in order to get foothold in a store. Patterson had to

send his first direct advertising matter in plain en-
velopes to keep it from the waste basket. To dishonest clerks the words "cash register" became
anathema.

The vicissitudes of the agents, who had now expanded to thirty, developed to the point where Patterson called them all in to Dayton for a conference
at the old Phillips House. This was the first known
sales meeting of the kind ever held and marked the
beginning of the NCR conventions which became a
feature of company selling. Patterson believed
firmly in the "get together" idea.

Despite all the opposition the salesmen made
progress. For the merchant they had, among other
things, the impregnable selling point:— "temptation
never takes a holiday." Clerks who wanted to ab-
stract cash from the open cash drawer required only
need and opportunity to fall.

An epoch in the art of selling began to unfold in
1887. The crack National Register salesman was
Joseph H. Crane, a brother-in-law of the Pattersons.
When he came in from one of his trips John H.
asked him:

"How do you sell so many registers?"

"I have built up a selling talk," replied Crane.

"How did you happen to do this?" queried Patterson, whereupon Crane made this response:

"It was like this. I had my machines in a hotel
room in Findlay, Ohio. Three prospects came in
succession but I failed to make a sale. Then I began

to think. I went back over my sales talks with the first prospect and remembered that I had overlooked some important points. I put them down on a pad. I did the same thing with the talks with the second and third prospects. I now had a complete selling talk. I got one of the prospects back to the hotel and, using the prepared talk, sold him a register."

"Suppose you try your talk on me," asked Patterson.

Crane delivered his talk. When he finished Patterson remarked:

"That talk would induce me to buy a cash register."

Then Patterson had an inspiration. He said: "I would like to have Frank hear your talk." Crane was agreeable, saying that since he made the talk half a dozen times every day one more made no difference. John H. got Crane out of the room on some pretext and hid a stenographer behind a screen. When Crane concluded his second rendition Patterson had a verbatim record of it. He knew its value and he capitalized it to the fullest extent.

Under John H.'s direction the Crane sales talk was made into a paper-back, typewritten booklet called the "The N.C.R. Primer" with the sub-title "How I Sell a Cash Register." So far as can be ascertained, this was the first canned sales talk. It was also the first sales manual. Patterson circulated it among the agents who were required then to memorize it. The unpretentious pamphlet embodied the so-called "verbatim approach and demonstration" still a potent force in selling. The Primer, therefore, was the cornerstone upon which a large part of the structure of modern sales education is reared. From it stemmed The National Cash Register Sales School, the quotas, points, Hundred Point conventions and guaranteed territories all to be disclosed in detail later in this narrative. The fact to be emphasized here is that John H. Patterson blazed the trail for sales training which helped to make salesmanship a science. He had the deeply rooted conviction that salesmen are not born, but made. The type of graduates of what became the NCR University of Business and their sales records, attest to the soundness of his theory.

Patterson's training technique was typical of the man. Always a realist, one of his first departures from conventional methods was to set up models of grocery, butcher and drug stores. He equipped them with dummy merchandise. The agents thus had a realistic setting for their sales talks. In the early days Patterson himself took the role of shopkeeper. This put the salesmen on their mettle. Out of this procedure developed the slogan "Know Your Store," an indispensable aid to selling. In the Patterson selling formula knowledge was always power.

Early Patterson set up his first list of "Don'ts" for salesmen. They included; don't do all the talking; don't advertise the register as a "thief catcher"; don't wait for a man to come to your office to buy; don't answer a question except with the truth. One other admonition was to urge agents to try to sell at night when there are fewer distractions for the merchant than during the day. Patterson also devised a plan for displaying registers on draped stands whether in hotel rooms or stores, so they would appear to best advantage. Here the showmanship in him asserted itself. Later it had larger play in the pageants, window displays, and conventions that he staged to dramatize selling and the progress of the business.

Patterson always insisted that his salesmen be well turned out. "You must sell yourself first," he always declared. Neat and scrupulously dressed himself, he demanded the same smartness in his representatives. He wanted the agents to broaden their horizons so he created what was then a unique plan. He sent the men on vacation trips to New York and insisted they purchase a wardrobe at his expense. There was more than the well-dressed man in this idea. Patterson wanted the agents to get the feel and satisfaction of spending. This gave them the incentive to sell more cash registers. His generosity was always practical.

Perhaps the most fundamental of the Patterson principles was summed up in the sentence, "We teach through the eye." This was eminently characteristic of the man and his philosophy of selling. He argued that instruction by ear goes in one ear and out the other, that most people do not listen attentively. He based his principle on the fact that the optic nerve is twenty-two times stronger than the auditory nerve and that the average person is more likely to remember what he sees than what he hears. Visualization in talking, teaching, and selling became a rule with him. From it developed his chalk talks on a blackboard and later the famous chart talks made with the aid of large sheets of paper mounted on a pedestal.

The origin of the pedestal reveals the Patterson resource and ingenuity. Early his vision beheld the whole world as a field for the cash register. After launching the business in England he decided to branch out in France. The first French employee was Jules Vuillaume who spoke good English. Patterson instructed him to rent a store and install some registers. The first problem was to get an audience so he told Vuillaume to ring a hand bell out on the street. This brought the populace flocking in. When the store was filled, he ordered the door locked.

Patterson now faced a dilemma. He said to Vuillaume:

"How can I demonstrate the register when I cannot speak a word of French?" As usual he met the emergency. He remembered his chalk talks to salesmen and executives in Dayton. Thereupon he commanded Vuillaume to get large sheets of paper and a crayon. With the sheets tacked on the wall he drew pictures that visualized the operations of the registers. Apparently the spectators understood what it was all about. That demonstration was the beginning of the NCR business in France. When Patterson returned to Dayton he had large sheets of paper attached to the top of a wooden stand. Each page could be turned over backward after it was filled. Such was the origin of the pedestal and the pedestal talks which, like so many Patterson innovations, remain in force wherever National machines are made and sold.

Under all the selling technique, stoked by training, rewards, and conventions which stimulated competition among the agents, the real march of the cash register began. The increase in monthly sales will indicate the progress. In April 1885 only 64 registers were sold. In April the following year 73 were installed, while April 1887 saw 164 new ones in stores. By 1887, 5400 machines were in operation. Three years later the list had grown to 16,395. National machines were reaching the ends of the world. Some were sold in picturesque circumstances. Agents on occasion risked life and limb to plant the product. The following is an instance:

An unsuccessful prospector came back disgusted from the Klondike gold rush. In Seattle he heard about the cash register. He went to Dayton and got the agency for all the territory north of the 60th Parallel which included part of the Arctic Circle. There was not a town within 1500 miles of his headquarters and no railroads. Transportation was only by dog sled and boat. The agent sailed from San Francisco with a stock of registers and arrived at

Cape Nome with his goods. Within two days he had sold the entire lot, many of which were delivered by dog team which cost him $10 an hour. He encountered icy hazards delivering the goods, and received payment in gold dust. When he returned to San Francisco he had $5,000 worth of the precious yellow stuff literally "in the bag."

Then, as always, Patterson saw the cash register not only as an indispensable aid to business but as a moral force as well. Hence his motto: "The more we sell the more good we do." Linked with this was the NCR yardstick, which is: Information, Protection, Service, Convenience, Economy, still the measure of National Cash Register service.

Re-enforcing the sales program was an avalanche of publicity. A zealot for advertising, Patterson launched the cash register on a sea of printers ink. Almost every conceivable medium through which the printed word could be used was mobilized for what became a continuous and cumulative campaign to stimulate selling.

The long list of house organs and kindred publications issued under the NCR standard is an illuminating example of how Patterson employed and deployed the printed word. The pioneer was called "Output," a single sheet which appeared in 1885. Its purpose was to give publicity to sales. Patterson went on the theory that sales make news, and that the news of sales makes for more sales. It reflected the angle of his technique of selling which always bore down hard on publicity. The announcement in the initial issue of "Output" that 22 registers were shipped in the week ending December 12th, 1885 was the vanguard of the flood of printed promotion that glorified the millionth sale in 1911 and all succeeding progressive high water selling marks. The "Output" was used mainly by salesmen with prospects. Before a year passed it had a contemporary in "The Hustler" which had four pages and supplemented the list of sales with news of the agents and the factory.

In "The Hustler" Patterson began his campaign of education with a department entitled "Points for Young Store Keepers on How to Run a Store." He showed pictures of the right and wrong way to deal with customers. He also presented pictures of shops in England, Holland, Sweden, Australia, and Germany that had installed registers. Among the earlier illustrations was one of a Zulu, clad only in loin cloth, operating a National register in Durban, Natal.

With the "N.C.R.," which made its debut in 1887, Patterson did some more pioneering in print. It was the first publication for circulation among the employees of any industrial organization in the United States. Originally devoted to the interests of sales agents, the columns were later expanded to cover the doings of all personnel at home and abroad. John H. Patterson edited "N.C.R." himself. His name appeared at the masthead of the second issue.

There was now the opportunity for capitalization

of another phase of the Patterson publicity creed. This phase was the extensive use of pictures. Patterson was an ardent disciple of the Chinese philosopher who said that "one picture is worth a thousand words." Henceforth, the "N.C.R." and every one of the many subsequent factory publications, whether newspaper, booklet, folder, advertisement, or poster, bristled with illustrations.

The "N.C.R." recorded many of Patterson's views and precepts. He devoted sections to store management and window dressing. Characteristically he gave ample space to "Health Hints" because "keeping fit" was a lifelong obsession with him. He had a "Corner of Clerks" in which he continued his advice to young men on how to succeed behind the counter. Soon he began to expand to factory news and plant activities. He started a camera contest and gave prizes for the best pictures. He published travelogues by employees and gave vacation hints. Behind all this flood of advice and counsel was the definite purpose of creating a community of useful interests.

No feature of "N.C.R.," however, so revealed the astute Patterson sense of sales stimulation as the continued publication of sales records. He not only printed the names of what he called "Banner Agents," those with the highest selling records, but emblazoned them on a banner in the center of the front page. Every agent was animated by a desire to get on the banner. The result was high-powered agent competition which meant increased business.

Patterson's frequent trips to Europe provided an abundance of good copy for "N.C.R." The introduction of the first advertising manager in 1889 relieved him of routine editorial work and gave him more freedom for travel. Patterson proved to be a good reporter for he always had fine powers of observation. His letters from Europe were full of meat and selling sense. It was natural that he should see European rulers in terms of business executives and countries like England, Germany, Russia, and France as "great commercial organizations." In a letter from Berlin toward the close of the eighties he wrote:

"I have been present when the head of one of these great organizations, the Czar of Russia, received his greatest rival, the Emperor of Germany, and showed him around his plant to illustrate to him how dangerous it would be for him to attempt to compete with that organization on its own ground."

Patterson's passion for house organs reached the point where two, and sometimes three, different types of publications were appearing simultaneously. In 1891 "Factory News" came along. Like all its sister NCR journals it combined sales promotion news with gossip of the plant and the workers. In 1933 it became the organ of the NCR family and still flourishes as such. As the years and the factory expanded the "National Cash Register," the "N.C.R. News," the "Agents Record" and the various papers published in connection with Hundred Point Conventions all played their part in fostering loyalty, sales, and publicity.

Save for the Probable Purchaser, the "P.P.," who bore the brunt of so much selling attack, these factory publications did not reach the general public. Patterson got his message over to them with generous newspaper and magazine advertising. He saw advertising as the fertilizer of the business field. His maxim was "Big Ideas and Little Words." The story is told that in the formative days of the company Patterson sent every piece of advertising copy over to a nearby German grocer to find out of he could understand it. "If this grocer can understand the advertisement, then everybody can," said Patterson.

All the Patterson advertising bore the stamp of utmost simplicity. Here is a sample advertisement which appeared in "The American Store-Keeper" of Chicago in August 1886 under the heading "What is a Cash Register?":

"It is an automatic cashier which records mechanically every cash or credit sale made in a store. It never tires. It never does one thing while thinking of another, and never makes a mistake. It is a mathematical prodigy in brass and steel, all of whose computations are infallibly correct. It is a machine which will save the money you make and thus pay for itself over and over again."

Patterson bore down hard on direct advertising and almost bankrupted himself in the early years for printing and postage. At one time he had 1,500,000 names on his merchants list. In a single year he sent out 18,500,000 pieces of direct advertising matter.

Acceleration of sales under Patterson's driving power necessitated larger factory quarters. Two years after he bought control of The National Cash Register Company he took over the entire third floor of the Callahan Power Building, retaining the original factory space as well. This area soon proved to be inadequate so Patterson decided to build his own plant.

The year 1888 set up a significant mile-post in the advance of the company for it saw the occupation of the first factory built exclusively for National cash register production. The site was part of the old Rubicon homestead where less than a decade before rows of corn had nodded in the wind. John H. Patterson came back to the farm, this time not to work the family land but to develop a great industry on it.

One preliminary to the construction of the factory was typical of Patterson's relations with his employees. He called the workmen together and told them of the factory project. He asked if they thought it would pay. All agreed that it would be a desirable move. He then said that the land had been platted and that various good home building locations would be available to them with no down payments, no interest, and a long period of time in which to pay. A number took advantage of the offer.

The new factory rose in exactly sixty days and was

occupied in June 1888 with 115 employees on the payroll. It was two and a half stories high and sixty by one hundred feet, giving five times the space in the original plant in the Callahan Power Building. Subsequently it was enlarged to become what is now Building Number One. In less than a month output increased from 20 to 25 registers a day. It is interesting to contrast that first factory with the community of production which is the NCR of today with 27 buildings, 30 acres of plant, and 56 acres of floor space. That roster of 115 workers in 1888 grew to 12,000 at the peak of the World War II effort when the company devoted the major part of its production to war work.

Not long before the move to the new factory Patterson figured in an incident thoroughly indicative of the man. A number of registers stood on benches ready for shipment. All had passed inspection except one. On that machine was a key that would not work. A workman had been instructed to repair it but he procrastinated.

Suddenly John H. Patterson entered the room with some guests to whom he was explaining the operation of registers. Pointing to the benches where the finished machines stood he said:

"Those registers have all been inspected and are ready to be shipped. I will show you how these machines work."

As ill luck would have it, Patterson stepped up to the one with the defective key and tried to operate it.

Of course it did not work. Turning to his guests he said:

"Here is one that doesn't work. Now I will show you what we do with registers that don't work properly."

With these words he placed the register on the floor, picked up a hammer laying nearby, and smashed the machine to bits.

Another episode at the original plant was more significant. It grew out of the return of a shipment of $50,000 worth of registers from England because of defective workmanship. It was a blow to prestige and profit. Patterson acted in his invariable realistic fashion. He moved his desk into the factory where he found out what was wrong. The factory was dark and dirty; the water for drinking and washing unclean. Discontent ruled at lathe and bench. Almost overnight he remedied the situation. The factory was cleaned. The men got lemonade instead of water. Each worker had his individual locker. The men were satisfied. No more registers came back. For one thing, this experience led Patterson to have all the walls of the NCR factories that followed 80 per cent glass. He was the pioneer in what is called the daylight factory.

Something larger and deeper than content and efficiency in work was wrought out of the incident that I have just related. Patterson learned that close contact with his employees was one of the bases of sound industrial relations. Henceforth he was the friend, philosopher, and guide of his workers.

In 1904 came the episode that influenced world industry. One day Patterson saw a woman warming a pot on a radiator. He naturally thought that it contained glue. Having an inquiring mind he investigated and found that it was coffee. It was the only hot feature of the midday meal of the female workers. It gave him the idea to provide hot meals for the women and later, all employees. This was the beginning of welfare in American industry. The hot meals were followed by baths on factory time, rest periods, dining rooms, medical service with a dental clinic, visiting nurses, health education, recreational grounds, motion pictures during lunch, garden clubs for employees, night classes and vacation and educational trips. Once more Patterson was the pathfinder.

During the first World War, I discovered how far-reaching was the welfare system established by Patterson. In 1915 I went out to visit the shell factory of Andre Citroen on the *Quai Javel* in Paris. Citroen was an obscure maker of ball bearings when the war started. Armed with some government contracts for shells he started a factory. Being alert and progressive he was on the way to becoming one of the munitions masters of France. With great pride he showed me a dental clinic in the plant. Knowing how backward most French industrial establishments were in the matter of welfare I asked him where he got the idea. He replied:

"I read about John H. Patterson's dental clinic in his cash register factory in Dayton and introduced it here. It has greatly increased the efficiency of the workers."

Patterson had a profound detestation of "yes, yes" men and was forever testing men to discover if they were chronically acquiescent. Early one snowy morning he called J. H. Barringer, then his secretary and later Vice-President and General Manager, into his office. As he shook the snow from the fur collar of his coat he pointed out the window and asked:

"Do you see the dog over there?"

"No," replied Barringer.

"Are you sure you do not see a dog?" queried Patterson.

"I am sure," responded the secretary.

Patterson gave a grunt of approval and the episode ended. There was no dog in the snow. The head of the company was checking his future Vice-President and General Manager to make certain he had a mind of his own.

Patterson had a high ideal of resource and service. In the determination to achieve his ideals he often wreaked his ruthless will. The phrase, "It can't be done," spelled instant dismissal for an employee. He hired and fired with almost lightning rapidity.

On one occasion he called in a foreman to get a report on the work in his department. The man said:

"I am glad to report that we are 100 per cent

efficient, the men are loyal and the best we can get. Our product is as perfect as can be made."

"Then you are perfectly satisfied," said Patterson.

"Yes, sir, I am."

"All right," retorted Patterson, "you are fired."

In the John H. Patterson code no one could ever be satisfied. He regarded satisfaction as akin to complacency. His ruling impulse was to stir men to better and bigger things. Here is an instance:

Few things pleased him more than to rally a rousing meeting of employees and give them a pep talk, or have some distinguished visitor do the pepping up. During a conference with workers he wrote the word "duke" on a chart. Then pulling a $10 bill out of his pocket he said:

"I will give this to anyone here who knows the origin and meaning of this word."

No one knew, so he said:

"That word comes from the Latin *duco* which means 'I lead.' You can all become leaders if you try hard enough; leaders at the bench; leaders in your section; leaders in your departments and offices."

While he drove men hard, he gave them ample compensation. At a meeting of supervisors, foremen and job foremen he once asked:

"How many of you have ever been to New York?"

Only a few held up their hands. Then he asked how many had been to Chicago and Washington, with the same result whereupon he said:

"You will all go."

The President gave instructions that the men be divided into groups, one to go to New York, another to visit Chicago, and a third to Washington at company expense. He exacted only two conditions. One was that they visit factories; the other that they write reports on their experiences and offer suggestions.

One event stands out pre-eminently in any estimate of John H. Patterson. It concerns the Dayton flood of March 1913 when the waters of the Miami, the Stillwater, and the Mad Rivers went on the rampage, inundating the city and bringing grief, loss and misery to a large part of the population. In that dark hour the Patterson genius for organization asserted itself to invoke the undying gratitude of a whole community.

As the angry, rain-swollen waters began to rise Patterson viewed the growing desolation from the roof of the NCR office building. He said:

"Dayton will have an awful flood today. We must prepare to house and feed the people who will be driven from their homes. I now declare the NCR temporarily out of commission and proclaim the Citizens Relief Committee."

The highly trained and flexible NCR organization went into action. By every available wagon, truck, and motor car Patterson rushed bedding, medicine, and hospital supplies to the plant. He ordered a special train-load of supplies from New York. He built boats, mobilized doctors, nurses, and relief workers. Thousands were rescued from their flooded houses and brought to the factory which expanded into a huge relief camp. Some of the children born at NCR during those trying days were named "Cash," the familiar designation of the company in Dayton. NCR Hill became Sanctuary Hill.

When officers of the Federal Government reached Dayton they said to Patterson:

"We can do nothing more than you have already done."

Those grim flood days that marked the high tide of Dayton's turbulent waters also marked the high tide of the Patterson humanitarianism. The waters receded but there was no recession in his public service.

The Patterson leadership did not end with the flood. Dayton lay prostrate under a sea of slime. Thousands of people, discouraged and disheartened over the ruin about them, wanted to leave the city. Again Patterson rose to the emergency. As head of the Citizens Relief Committee he urged the people to remain and redeem the community. He helped to rekindle the fires of their faith. Dayton rose reborn from the ordeal to fulfill her destiny.

Patterson had little regard for so-called higher education. He maintained that although he studied Greek, Latin, and Higher Mathematics at Dartmouth, his college professors never trained him to acquire a good memory. He always carried a little red book in his pocket containing a list of "Things

James Ritty
Inventor of the cash register

The first cash register

The latest model National Cash Register

The NCR plant from the air

Col. E. A. Deeds (left) and S. C. Allyn

Scene in one of the NCR factory buildings

The new London building is the headquarters of the British organization

NCR Employees with factory in the background

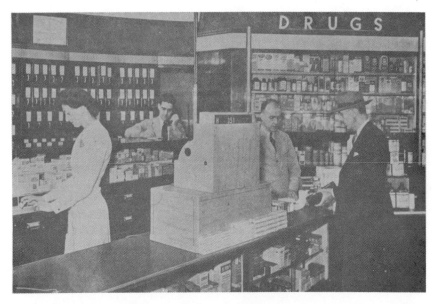

In this drug store a multiple drawer National Cash Register gives complete information on sales by departments and by salespeople

A National Cash Register provides an efficient means of gaining complete control of fountain sales

to Do." At Christmas time he sent thousands of these books to his friends and employees. He further devised a plan to aid memory by grouping his thoughts. He used five, since, he said, you have five toes, five fingers, and five senses. All his bulletins, pyramids, and pamphlets were presented in five headings.

The use of the pyramid was a demonstration of teaching through the eye. Patterson broke down practically everything he discussed from an idea to an organization, in pyramid form. He was almost inarticulate without recourse to a pedestal on which he could write or draw as he talked. He took a pedestal along wherever business led him. He carried this means of expression to the extreme of having a pedestal installed in his bedroom frequently employing it to chart thoughts that came to him during sleepless hours. The pedestal is still in use in every executive office in the Dayton factory and in all branches where National machines are made or sold.

There were few periods in the development of the company when Patterson did not order some drastic change or revision in personnel or operation. He could never remain static. Once he cabled from England:

"The Board of Directors must be enlarged to thirty."

A high ranking executive in Dayton wired back:
"The law provides for only fifteen directors."

Quickly the reply came from Patterson:
"Change the law."

The change could be effected only by Act of the Ohio State Legislature but it was put through. Patterson found, however, that thirty directors were a trifle unwieldy. The company returned to the old order but Ohio law still permits thirty directors in a Corporation.

While never robust, Patterson was a stickler for exercise, especially riding. He was an expert horseman and rode every morning before going to his office. At one time he insisted that all the executives of the company take up riding. It was another manifestation of his obsession that employees should keep fit.

Patterson did not deviate from the daily horseback ride during his travels abroad. He carried half a dozen riding outfits and had a list of riding academies where suitable mounts could be obtained in every important European capital. Dr. F. G. Barr, his personal physician for years and now head of industrial relations at NCR, accompanied him on most of his trips and rode with him daily.

On one occasion Patterson and Dr. Barr arrived in Berlin early in the morning from Sweden. Within an hour they were at Tattersalls, the largest riding academy in the German capital. The riding master brought out four horses, one of which was spirited and high strung. Patterson immediately selected him as his mount. The riding master said to Dr. Barr in German:

"That horse is a dangerous animal and requires a skillful rider. I advise your friend not to ride him."

Patterson, who spoke no German, asked Dr. Barr what the man had said. The moment he heard it he leaped on the spirited horse, put him through the paces in the riding ring, and dashed out for a gallop in the Tiergarten, the huge park in the center of Berlin. He was always proud of his horsemanship. The monument to his memory in Dayton shows him on his favorite horse Spinner.

I had an experience with Patterson's passion for getting his friends to ride when I first visited him at Far Hills, his estate just outside Dayton. Soon after I arrived he asked me if I rode. When I told him that I had never been on a horse he said:

"Now, now, (this was his usual way of beginning a sentence) that will not do. You must learn how to ride while you are here."

I wanted to sit in comfort while I was his guest and gently demurred. Patterson was insistent. The next morning a groom with an extra horse turned up and I began my career as horseman.

Fame and fortune did not impair the simplicity which was part of Patterson's heritage. Nor did he forget the days when he drudged on the farm. The Pattersons held a high position in Dayton society but John H. was absolutely without ostentation or

social ambition. Social prestige meant little in his
life as this incident shows:

Patterson's sister, Mrs. Julia Crane, wanted a
family crest and confided the ambition to her
brother. Much to her surprise he acquiesced readily
to the idea, saying that they would do something
about it when they were next in New York. A few
months later they met in New York and went to
Tiffany's famous store on Fifth Avenue. When the
head of the engraving department asked Patterson if
he had any ideas for a crest he replied:

"Oh, yes. I suggest a coal bucket rampant on a
plow."

The crest business ended then and there.

Patterson was often misunderstood, opposed, and
criticized. One reason was that his vagaries were
many. Often it was difficult to understand the reasons
for his acts. He was swift to reward and equally
quick to condemn. Justice is a harsh task mistress
and he believed that he always obeyed her behests.

Like many outstanding men of big vision Patterson was ahead of his time. He formulated principles
and practices that are basic in American business.
He had the rare quality of leadership which made
him an industrial prince. With his sponsorship and
development of the cash register he added a domain
to the empire of production. He did not live to see
the wizardry of accounting machine expansion
which the company fostered after his death, yet here,

as elsewhere in the concern which was his pride
and joy, his teachings go marching on.

In 1921 Patterson relinquished the presidency of
the company and became Chairman of the Board.
His son Frederick B., succeeded him as President.
Patterson continued his active connection with the
company and likewise with his ramified outside interests which ranged from the civic betterment of
Dayton to the League of Nations in Geneva.

The end came to Patterson May 7th, 1922 in circumstances characteristic of his active life. He
died on a train bound for Atlantic City where he
had planned to spend a brief holiday. All Dayton
mourned him as her foremost citizen.

The National Cash Register Company is John H.
Patterson's monument. His epitaph might well be
a declaration which he once made to a group of
associates:

"If ever there comes a time in this business when
courage is not needed, when it is not necessary to
overcome obstacles, I will know that it is time to
close down, turn off the power, and draw the fires
for all time."

CHAPTER III

The Evolution of the Cash Register

FROM the start of the Patterson regime the rule—"We Progress Through Change"—has influenced every phase of NCR production. Born in a Century of Progress, John H. Patterson followed its dominant dictate which became a mandate for his successors. The course of the National cash register, therefore, has been a continuous process of change always with the objective of increased efficiency and an ever-widening field.

Beginning as an inanimate policeman, the cash register has been developed to the stage where it is adapted to every type and kind of business whether for service or merchandising. Few other kinds of machines carry such a moral implication. The cash register remains the keeper of the business conscience. Its calculating devices, with myriad springs, gears, rolls, levers, and shafts reaching metal fingers into untold places accomplish the desired result by many and devious combinations. Accuracy, dependability, and longevity are the essential requirements. They must account for the last penny, make the correct computations, and print the amount in the designated place.

The paper roll machine devised by James Ritty had 375 parts. Today one of the most highly developed National registers—the class 6000—contains 7,716 parts. These intricate parts command the varied services of the research engineer. The metallurgist must determine the proper steel and other metals to provide hardness, toughness, and durability. The chemist is called upon to provide inks, printing plates, ribbon, and paper.

With the discovery of new principles, processes, and materials fresh horizons are opening for their application in electronics, chemistry particularly with plastics, and design. Constant research is to the cash register what fuel is to the motor car. Stop it and production, like the car, would coast on for a while but the point of inertia would soon be reached. Eternal research is the price of advance.

Behind the research engineer stands the inventor who must chart the path of progress. Cash registers are not evolved with hope and a prayer. Their birth, adolescence, and maturity are carefully planned. Before every type of National machine is designed and patented, and long before it goes on the market, the Company knows it will sell. It knows, also, that it will stand up against the ordeal of climate. Machine resistance to humidity and salt air is tested in Florida and Panama. Millions of dollars and years of patient and painstaking effort are expended upon

the development of a single type of register. It requires five years to perfect a machine. Moreover,
the product must be foolproof because it must not
be susceptible to careless mis-operation, and fraud-
proof since it must resist attempts by a dishonest
clerk to "beat" it. Preventive construction is the
preventive medicine of this industry. In sixty years
NCR has taken out 2400 patents. The expansion of
the cash register confirms the theory that an invention is not a creation but a growth.

In the NCR pioneering days there were no inventors to improve the product. The early developments came about largely through rectifying complaints from users. This was the far-away beginning
of a policy which has animated the Company ever
since. It grows out of the fact that the customer,
not through complaint but through his needs and
suggestions, has become, in a sense, one of the arbi-
ters of machine development. The agency through
which needs and suggestions are translated into
action is called Product Development.

Product Development is the link between Engineering, the Sales Field, and the users of machines.
It is a melting pot of ideas out of which emerge improvements and new models. The scout of Product
Development is the salesman who, by contact with
the customers, learns their needs and relays them to
the factory in Dayton. They are first referred to a
Field Committee of salesmen whose acid test is,
"Has it sales appeal?" Another function of Product

Development and salesmen, and through them the users, is to devise new applications for machines in use. The flexibility of the National product permits it to be tailored to constantly increasing uses.

Coordinating Engineering and Production is Carl H. Kindl who brings a long factory experience to this all important task. He must reconcile complicated mechanical differences, keep pace with research, and watch the pulse of invention. A graduate of the Carnegie Institute of Technology he reached a Vice Presidency in NCR by way of the Delco Products Division of the General Motors Corporation.

Part of the evolution of the cash register can best be revealed in the improvements that have developed in quick succession. Each one established a little epoch of progress. Together they have combined for the last word in efficiency and service. Progressively they have contributed to a transformation in bookkeeping and merchandising.

You will recall that James Ritty introduced the indicator and the detail adder which replaced the paper roll with rotating numbered wheels. To find the total amount of business done it was necessary to add the totals shown by each adding wheel. Before long there were self-adding wheels. In turn came the Total Adder machine which enabled the merchant to tell at a glance the total of all sales "rung up." This was the forerunner of the many sizes and models of National totalizer registers. At this juncture an important innovation arrived with the press-in key which made for a larger degree of key control. The press-in key is today a feature of all highly developed National machines.

The next step in National cash register progress, the detail strip, showed how merchant needs have been met. Shopkeepers wanted information about individual sales. The detail strip supplies this need because it records each transaction chronologically. Among other things it enables the proprietor to check the operator through test purchases for odd amounts made by an outsider. He can then discover if all sales are recorded. The detail strip also serves as an audit strip for bookkeeping records.

The early 90's were marked by the introduction of a notable addition to National cash register service. It was the receipt which permitted the merchant to give his customers a printed record of the sale in addition to having his own record on the detail strip. The receipt established another definite mile-post because it provides protection for customer, merchant, and clerk. For one thing it makes the customer the auditor of the transaction and thus promotes customer confidence.

The receipt achieves a four-fold benefit. It assists the customer in getting correct change; enables him to identify merchandise returned; protects him in case the merchandise is brought by messenger or servant, and removes temptation if the purchase is made by children who are inclined to spend change for soda or sweets on the way home. Under the receipt system the merchant gets the exact amount spent by the customer because each sale is added in a locked total which checks the contents of the drawer at the close of the day's business. Finally, the receipt gives the clerk the opportunity to prove his honesty in every sale he makes. The receipt, as we all know, has also become an agency for good will and publicity for the store. It contains the name and address of the establishment, the date and record of sale, and a "Thank you—Call Again."

Some people are inclined to say: "Why take a receipt? The floors of shops are littered with them." The answer is simple. The more receipts on the floor, the more money in the register drawer. The clerk does not know whether you have looked at the receipt or not, but he does know that the amount recorded on it has been rung up and that there must be an accounting for it.

The National cash register now remedied a long standing ill in merchandising. Many merchants were forced to write out sales slips because of the types of merchandise they carried and particularly with charge sales. The sales slip was subject to constant manipulation. There was no way of knowing that because a slip was written out, the shop-keeper got the money for it. A machine was devised which printed the amount of the sale on the main portion of an inserted sales slip and also on the stub of the slip which was cut off by the register and deposited in a locked box. This machine inaugurated the use of National cash registers in department stores, as you will presently see.

Once more a pressing merchant need was met in an improvement that set up still another bulwark of protection. When more than one clerk handled money in the register drawer responsibility for mistakes or abstractions could not be fastened on any single person. Obviously if John Smith was responsible for cash in the drawer, then only John Smith should have access to it. This led to the development of the multiple drawer machine in which each clerk has his or her drawer. Some machines have as many as nine drawers. A further safeguard is that each drawer rings a bell different in sound from any of the other bells. If a clerk in a distant part of the store hears his bell rung he knows that his drawer is open.

Merchants liked the multiple drawer feature but recognized that more service was required of the register. When cash was out of balance it was necessary to separate each clerk's sales on the detail audit strip and total them in order to find out how much cash should be in each drawer. This was slow and inconvenient. Multiple counters were then invented to determine the sales of each clerk. Another innovation was that there were now separate totals for such items as Cash, Charge, Received on Account, and Paid Out.

When the four items just mentioned first appeared

on a National cash register mechanized bookkeeping may be said to have begun. To no user of these registers was the improvement more welcome than the corner grocery man and kindred merchants who could not afford to employ a bookkeeper. They kept their own books with the consequence that oversight in recording "Paid out" often resulted in paying a bill twice; that failure to credit a customer who paid on account lost both customer and money. Hence the improved machine was a Godsend to the little man and to others as well.

During all this evolution the improvement of the outside of the register kept pace with the development of the mechanism inside. The first National registers were put out in wooden cabinets. Later the cabinets were made of ornamental brass. They were cumbersome affairs, ornate with the decorative agony of the Victorian era. People in those days wanted that kind of equipment. Often the name of the owner of the register was conspicuously displayed on a heavy metal plate. He wanted publicity for himself as well as for sales. Gradually the showy cabinets began to give way to simple designs. Today the National cash register cabinet is streamlined, made of metal with a finish to resemble wood.

Meanwhile the United States was becoming increasingly electrically minded. Surprising gadgets were springing up to lighten the burden of labor. Then, as always, NCR stood in the van of progress. "The cash register must be operated by electricity," was the new mandate. It would replace the crank that had come into use to facilitate operation and provide speed and convenience.

There was a big gap, however, between the wish for a motor on the cash register and fulfillment. It was not an ordinary problem of operating a machine by electricity. The difficulties are evident by a comparison with the motor drive of a washing machine. In the electric operation of a washing machine it does not matter what position the moving parts are in when the motor begins to whirl. It is also immaterial as to what position the parts are left when the current is turned off. This is not true of a cash register. All its parts are in a definite position before it is operated and they must be back in their places when the transaction is completed. They cannot be left in an intermediate position. Despite the arguments of experts that a cash register motor was an impossibility, a motor for this purpose was designed at the NCR factory. It was necessary, however, to perfect it. The need for this development found the man in Charles F. Kettering.

On a boiling hot day in the summer of 1904 Kettering turned up at the factory and took over a desk and bench in what was called "Inventions 3." He was lank, gangling, spectacled, and talked with an Ohio back country drawl. There was a good deal of the dirt farmer about him and with good reason, for he had been born on a farm two and a half miles from Loudonville, Ohio. From his earliest boyhood the hunger for knowledge stirred him to almost incessant study. He walked the five miles to and from the Loudonville High School and found time for the farm chores. In his early school days he was torn between a love of Greek and a passion for physics with physics usually getting the better of the conflict.

Kettering had barely reached his 'teens when he revealed his instinct for mechanical research. With fourteen dollars, the first money he ever earned by cutting a neighbor's wheat crop, he bought a telephone from a mail order house. Within twenty-four hours it was completely dissected. He always wanted to know how and why things worked. His operations on the family sewing machine almost drove his mother to distraction. That inquiring mind of his was to speed him to the great places.

After teaching school at Mifflin, Ohio where he tinkered with chemicals and machines in the back room of a friend's drug store at night, Kettering became a student in electrical engineering at Ohio State University at Columbus. His nest egg was the meager left-over from his earnings as pole-setter in an Ohio telephone gang. He was not the type of student selected by classmates "as the one most likely to succeed." The homespun quality, which later contributed so much to his charm, apparently did not operate in his favor at college. Besides, unlike many of his fellow students, he did not have an aversion to work.

Kettering's spare frame was deceptive for, at the university, and in the succeeding years, he was animated by what has been called "a ferocious energy." It drove him through the early years of work and study and it became a prime asset when he took his place in "Inventions 3" at the NCR factory. His simple and unaffected manner, his fervor for work—he never knew the meaning of a time clock—and his flair for leadership, made for instant popularity. Overnight he became "Boss Ket." Despite wealth, achievement, and a multitude of honors he remains "Boss Ket" to those old colleagues and to the long list that came later on with his expanding field of effort.

It took Kettering three years to confute the experts who had maintained that a cash register motor was a mechanical impracticability. The motor was revolutionary in that it largely supplanted the old crank operation on the register. Both motor and crank were put on machines, in case the electric current failed. The operator could still apply the crank and make the register manually operated until the current was restored.

Once installed, electrification justified the confidence of its NCR promoters. It produced the speed and convenience which they knew would result. The motor helped to increase the efficiency of the long line of improved registers and accounting machines that followed its installation.

Another assignment was put on Kettering's desk.

It developed from an urgent need in department stores where already National registers were strongly entrenched. An archaic system of authorizing credit had been in operation for years. Charge accounts were mainly checked by telephone. At that time telephones were not as numerous as now. The clerk was obliged to go to a wall telephone usually some distance from the sales counter, and call the credit office, or send the charge slip by mechanical messenger. The credit authorizer then telephoned approval or disapproval of the charge sale. Meanwhile delay, impatience, and sales interruption resulted. Merchants said to NCR:

"You have given us a system to protect cash sales. What we need now is a faster method of authorizing credit and eliminating the delays of the mechanical messenger."

This was the problem laid in Kettering's lap. He attacked it in his usual direct way for he went to the leading department store in Dayton to see what happened when a charge sale was authorized. After watching the performance he found his clue. He said: "Why not tie up the telephone directly with the sale?"

The result was the O. K. Telephone, an electrical system which enables the clerk to get quick authorization on a credit sale. The clerk puts the sales slip into a stamping device on the counter. She then calls the credit authorizer over a telephone attached to the device, and tells her the name of the customer and the amount to be charged. The credit clerk, whose records are at her elbow, looks up the customer's rating. It the sale is to be authorized she presses a button and the O. K. is stamped on the slip. A negative verdict is recorded the same way. The time of the operation is cut to a minimum.

By the time the Twentieth Century had rounded out its first decade NCR registers presented an imposing array of varied service. The National machine was now an acknowledged systematizer of business and a gleaner and recorder of the information so essential to its successful conduct. Merchants had come to realize that without a register and the information it assembled they were, as NCR sales agents put it, "like a man blindfolded."

In 1921 emerged the machine that expressed the highest type of register yet perfected. It was the so-called class 2000, embodying all features of past registers and accomplishing results that heretofore would have necessitated the use of several registers of different types. It met the needs of business for which no other machine would be adequate. The class 2000 has counters for 27 individual transactions and three group totals. In addition, it includes an autographic type of detail strip which permits the entry of any written memorandum or notation that may be desirable. Its great flexibility lends itself to the handling of intricate retail transactions.

The 6000, an offshoot of the 2000, is also revolutionary because of its adaptability for use in self service, that is, "check-out," food stores, drug stores, cafeterias and other establishments where a variety of items must be recorded. Hence it is known as an "itemizer" because it literally lists and adds different items. In addition to mechanical computation this register publicizes to the customer, the merchant, the clerk, and everyone within sight of the machine, the exact amount charged for each item. This feature enables the store manager and other supervisory agents to check on the accurate recording of constantly changing prices and therefore instills in the customer a complete confidence that the exact amount of each item is registered.

An epoch in NCR history opened with the introduction of the class 2000. The 30 totals made it possible for the machine to be adapted to uses other than retail business. The 2000 became a Mother of Machines. From it sprang the lusty line of NCR accounting machines which developed a field of almost bewildering service which simplifies and expedites the business of hotels, railroads, banks and industries as well as retail stores. The NCR accounting machines and their manifold services rate a chapter all their own.

It is difficult to find a business activity in which a National cash register does not find a place. The retail store was the starting point for a diffusion of service that touches railroads, universities, hospitals, toll bridges, Municipal and County Treasurers, Registers of Deeds, doctor, taxicab, and sheriff offices, golf courses, public service corporations, opticians, cooperative societies, funeral homes, Clerks of Municipal Courts, clinics, steamship lines, newspaper counting rooms, clubs, ferries, laundries, restaurants, dairies, poultry farms, in fact wherever money is handled. One of the most unique settings for a National cash register is the Commissary Store in Vatican City. When attendance at Worlds Fairs is recorded so that the public may follow admissions a huge model of a cash register is set up. So too, with the War Loan drives. A mammoth model of a National register in Times Square, New York City, recorded the progress of patriotic buying.

We can now turn from machines to men behind the machines. In 1899 there entered upon the NCR scene the man destined to exert an influence on Company policy and expansion second only to that exercised by John H. Patterson. He was Edward A. Deeds.

The Deeds story is in the best American tradition. Born on a farm near Granville, Ohio, like John H. Patterson, the pioneer strain is in his blood for his grandparents on both sides came out to Ohio by wagon from the East. Deeds had the usual farm boyhood alternating between studies at the Licking County District School and work on the land. An instinct for science was early manifest so he enrolled as a science student at Denison University. He could not afford to live in the college town so he rode the five miles to Denison every day on a horse. This permitted him to continue his farm work. In 1897 he received his degree of Bachelor of Science.

While Deeds was growing up, Dayton was also expanding in stature. The town had become a magnet for young Ohioans who wanted factory jobs, so Deeds joined the procession. He got a position as engineer in the Thresher Electric Company at $6 a week. On his arrival in Dayton he found that Mrs. Thresher, a motherly soul, had engaged a room with board for him. It was a kind and thoughtful act. The trouble was that it cost his full week's pay. Deeds thereupon rented a room for $4 a week. In order to save the 25 cents cost of transporting his trunk to the new abode he borrowed a wheelbarrow and trundled it over himself on his first Sunday in town.

The Thresher plant was small but its compactness was an asset for young Deeds. He mastered every detail of work in the place. Within a year he was superintendent and Chief Engineer.

The year 1899 stands out in the Deeds career because it saw him enrolled at the NCR as construction and maintenance engineer. At 25 he was shy, tallish, with broad shoulders and a sturdy frame. His blue eyes were observant and he was a good listener. Thus he had two assets essential to success. Deeds had played full back and tackle on the Denison football team and in his last collegiate year was captain of the eleven. He had done some stout tack-

ling as footballer. The experience helped to equip
him for the job he tackled at NCR.

Within six months Deeds revealed his resource in
an episode that became an oft-told tale at NCR and
eventually brought him to the attention of John H.
Patterson. It evolved about the smokestack that tow-
ered 175 feet above the NCR factory. The stack had
an outer shell and an inner core with an air space
between. The air space, however, had been continued only to within 34 feet of the top. At this point
the air space opened through ventilators to the interior. The inner core and outer shell extended to
the top coping as a solid wall. Inside the chimney
was an iron ladder that reached to the top. These
technical explanations are necessary to an understanding of what Deeds did.

One day Deeds noticed that there was something
wrong at the top of the stack. He examined the place
through a field glass and looked up the drawings of
the chimney. He became convinced that some of the
bricks were loose and might topple off to endanger
life and property. At that time Frank Patterson was
Factory Manager and Chairman of the Factory
Committee. When Deeds reported his observation
to him he said:

"That stack was built by engineers who have put
up more chimneys than you have ever seen."

Deeds was not to be daunted. On the following
Sunday when the furnaces were idle but the bricks
of the stack were still hot, he went to work. With

foundry gloves on his hands and a wet sponge over his nose, he climbed the iron ladder to the top of the stack through clouds of soot. He saw loose bricks and photographed them. The following day he hired a rigger. Between them they fashioned a bo'swains chair. Once more Deeds climbed the ladder to the top of the stack and then swung the chair on the outside so he could make a thorough examination of the exterior. He was now able to take out some of the loose bricks. He went to Frank Patterson again but this time "with the goods." When he saw the bricks Patterson said:

"I apologize. Whatever you do in this plant hereafter will have my full support."

What had happened was perfectly clear. The inner core being hotter, had expanded more than the outer shell and lifted the solid part of the stack at the top, causing a crack and the bricks to be loosed. The cause was simple but the remedy difficult. To rebuild the entire stack would have meant stoppage of factory work. To separate the two walls at their junction would have been hazardous because the outer wall could not support the weight unaided. Deeds decided to build a heavier outer shell.

The old shell was removed, leaving the core standing when near disaster broke. A heavy wind storm sprang up wrecking the scaffolds and precipitating 90 feet of brick work through the powerhouse roof on top of the boilers. Steel beams and steam pipes became a twisted mass of wreckage.

The storm broke at eight o'clock in the evening. Deeds mobilized a crew and, working all through the night, set up an emergency steam plant out of the debris which functioned so well that the factory whistle blew as usual the next morning. There was no interruption in work.

From the time of the smokestack episode Deeds was regarded as an up and coming man in the organization. Frank Patterson became his friend and ally. He once showed his friendship in an amusing incident. Deeds rode to and from the factory on a bicycle. One night his lamp went out unobserved by him, and he was arrested for violation of a city ordinance. Over his protests he was taken to the police station and signed the blotter.

In those days NCR executives lunched at an Officers Club. Deeds was the first to arrive the day after this episode. As practical jokers all the executives carefully avoided the table where Deeds sat. When Patterson came in he went over and took a seat alongside Deeds saying:

"I have signed the same blotter. Pay no attention to these men. You and I will form a society of our own."

In 1901, when he was 27 years old, Deeds became Chief Engineer in charge of Design and Construction at the Shredded Wheat plant at Niagara Falls where he designed and installed the machinery for electric baking. This, and other equipment, represented a distinct innovation in food production.

Deeds returned to NCR in 1902 as Vice President and Assistant General Manager. At first he occupied himself, as before, with engineering and construction. He planned the NCR branch factories in Canada and Germany. By this time National registers had become world citizens.

The unwavering confidence that Deeds had in the application of electricity to industry now had ample justification. It was he who not only conceived the idea of a motor on a cash register, but designed and built the first one to be put on a cash register. It was Deeds, too, who brought Kettering into the NCR fold.

Deeds wanted a bright young electrical engineer to whom the electrification project could be entrusted. He wrote to Alfred D. Cole, his old professor of physics at Denison, who had joined the faculty of Ohio State University, to suggest a likely candidate. Cole replied:

"I know the man for the job. He is Charles F. Kettering, one of my students. You cannot get him, however, because a position with a telephone company is open to him."

Undeterred, Deeds wrote to Kettering offering him a position at $50 a week. Kettering accepted but said that until the end of the term he could only come to Dayton for weekends. He was finishing up his university course. Deeds started his salary at once. When Kettering turned up at the NCR factory after the second week he pulled one of the company

checks for $50 out of his pocket and handed it to
Deeds with the remark:

"There has been a clerical mistake. I got two
checks for $50."

Kettering, with his mind concentrated on science,
had not read the Deeds letter carefully and believed
that he was to get $50 a month. To a young man who
had been teaching school and working as pole-setter
this was a lot of money.

Thus was established the contact between Deeds
and Kettering which had momentous consequences.
They had much in common. To engineering minds
they brought vision, resource, and energy. These
qualities were soon mobilized for the appliance
which electrified the motor car and made its use universal. The first step was the development of a
single spark battery ignition system which led the
way for the self-starter.

The approach to this epoch-making invention was
interesting. From its early day the automobile had
intrigued Deeds. At one time he had an ambition to
go into motor car production. He realized, however, that it was too big for him to swing on his own.
He then reasoned that if he could not produce cars
he could, as he expressed it, "put something on cars."
He confided his desire to Kettering who became his
devoted ally. Henceforth they worked in closest
collaboration.

Obviously it was necessary to have a car to work
on. Deeds had built one with his own hands in the

frame barn behind the house he then occupied on Central Avenue in Dayton. This car, and Kettering's Cadillac roadster, which was the main guinea pig, rated a place in the Smithsonian Museum because they were the fourwheel laboratories out of which emerged the electric ignition and starting system on automobiles. One tangible outcome of the Deeds-Kettering team work was the Dayton Engineering Laboratories Company, soon to be contracted into Delco, which became synonymous with motor car electrification and farm lighting plants.

In 1909 Kettering, who had worked in the NCR by day and toiled in the Deeds barn by night and Sundays, forsook "Inventions 3" to devote himself to research and invention. At the start the men behind Delco had no intention of going into production. The laboratories were to be an "idea factory." The pressure of events soon disrupted this plan. Kettering was launched on the career that led him to industrial and scientific eminence. Deeds went his way to achieve a more varied but equally constructive life work. The link between Deeds and Kettering has never been broken for today Kettering, the one-time $50 a week inventor, working in the obscurity of "Inventions 3," sits on the Board of Directors of the NCR.

In 1913 Deeds became identified with the project that was to rear an enduring monument to his public service. It concerns the aftermath of the Dayton flood. Even before the wreckage had been cleared from the streets far-seeing men were saying: "This must never happen again." Through the Citizens Relief Committee funds were raised and engineers employed to study the problem of flood control for the Miami Valley. The movement demanded leadership. Soon it centered in Deeds.

Flood control involved the enactment of a conservancy law because Ohio did not have a statute that would permit a cooperative undertaking of this nature. It was also necessary to set up a conservancy district and to take the legal steps preliminary to construction. By 1915 the Miami Conservancy District had been established with Deeds as President and a member of the Board of Directors.

Bitter agitation that revived memories of Copperhead Days in our Civil War marked what developed into the battle for flood control. When legal and legislative obstacles had been hurdled, human barriers rose up to impede action. Farmers in the Miami Valley, forgetting the travail of the flood, opposed the project because they believed it was for the sole benefit of the large communities. Furthermore, they resented condemnation and assessment of their property.

Deeds was in the forefront of the fight. Day and night he went up and down the Valley exhorting the farmers to see the light. Windows in the halls where he spoke were broken; his life was threatened more than once. He and his associates kept to their task. At the height of the agitation he built the structure in

Dayton that houses the offices of the Miami Valley Conservancy District at his own expense. It was his evidence of faith in the project expressed in stone. Flood control for the Miami Valley became a reality in 1924. Twice since the completion of the work it has withstood high waters that would have caused disastrous floods. Representing a total expenditure of $35,000,000 it ranks as the world's outstanding flood control project.

Due to his increasing outside business interests Deeds retired from NCR in 1914. The flood control project represents a localized public service. Soon he was to contribute his gifts to an activity that held the national, and beyond that, the international stage.

For some years Deeds had been a close friend of his fellow Daytonian, Orville Wright. Aviation fascinated him for he saw its immense possibilities. Before the First World War broke, Deeds realized the inevitability of our participation and the urgent need of American preparedness especially in the air. When we were committed to the struggle, it was natural that he should be called to Washington where his experience as successful executive and manufacturer of highly technical apparatus, combined with his vision and energy, could be utilized in our air program. We had only a meager few fighting and training planes and our aviation industry scarcely existed. We were obliged to start practically from scratch.

As Chief of Aircraft Procurement with the rank

of Colonel, Deeds sponsored and brought about the development and production of the Liberty engine in the face of almost heartbreaking delay and difficulty. When the armistice stilled the great guns 20,475 Liberty engines had been produced and many were in service abroad, all within the period of a year. History will record that Colonel Deeds, as father of the Liberty engine, made a definite contribution to the advancement of commercial and military aviation in this country.

Obviously the NCR is part of the Deeds destiny because in 1931 he returned, this time as Chairman of the Board of Directors. The circumstances that brought about his return revealed the regard and admiration in which he was held not only at the NCR factory but throughout Dayton. As head of the flood control project and in other public movements he had established himself as civic leader. His departure had left a gap. Dayton wanted that gap filled. A committee of NCR directors went to New York and extended the invitation that brought him back.

The Deeds homecoming, for such it was, reflected the deep affection of his associates. He found his old office precisely as he had left it in 1913. It made him feel that he had never gone away. With the retirement of Frederick B. Patterson as President in 1936 he assumed that office. Four years later he relinquished the presidency but remains Chairman of the Board.

When Colonel Deeds took over the chief NCR

executive post he brought to it a many-sided equipment. He was an industrialist of long experience and he was also engineer, inventor, and financier. He had a complete grasp of the business from the power house up, and he had a rare knowledge of men born of varied contact. These qualifications have enabled him to function as master builder and master negotiator. Hence Company policy and future development are among his responsibilities. His sturdiness of character has the flavor of the soil from which he sprang. It makes for the simplicity which is part of his heritage. Calm and unruffled, he has never been known to raise his voice regardless of provocation. Endowed with a deep spiritual nature, he brings soul to industry.

Like most men of achievement Colonel Deeds has the great gift of concentration. When he returned to NCR in 1931 he sat on the boards of 28 corporations ranging from Cuban sugar to the most powerful bank in the United States. In the intervening years Colonel Deeds has retired from most of the outside boards. One of the few directorships that he retains is on the board of the National City Bank of New York. Indicative of his energy is the fact that every week with few exceptions for fourteen years he has commuted to New York from Dayton to attend the board meeting.

The Deeds sense of humor has enabled him to cope with many difficult situations. Nowhere is his humor more happily revealed than at the daily luncheons in the Horseshoe Room at the factory over which he presides. This room is a distinctive NCR institution for it is a cross-section of industrial democracy. At the long table, shaped like a horseshoe which enables everybody literally to "get together," gather the executives, heads of departments, supervisors, and foremen. Often there is a distinguished guest who makes an informal talk. Colonel Deeds' introduction of these visitors, and the many talks he makes at factory meetings, bristle with wit, anecdote, and amusing reminiscence.

The Deeds mastery of many subjects has become an NCR tradition. I once heard "The Colonel," as he is affectionately called by his colleagues as well as by factory personnel, deliver a talk in the Horseshoe Room on the Miami Valley flood control project. Into a single hour, and in simple language, he compressed every detail of the big undertaking. When he concluded you would have thought that he had devoted his entire active life to hydraulic engineering.

The career of Colonel Deeds reveals the big vision which is one of his great qualities. He comprehends the prerogatives of labor and likewise the responsibilities of management, welding them into the harmonious entity which is the NCR family. He personifies industrial statesmanship.

Fourteen years after Colonel Deeds first entered the NCR service Stanley C. Allyn's name went on the payroll at $20 a week. These two men, then at almost opposite poles on the Company organization chart, were destined for an association that has made for a rare leadership.

In Allyn you have once more a typical American success story that only lacks the farm background. Born in Madison, Wisconsin, he is the son of a manufacturer of farm implements. As a boy he had a carrier route for the Chicago Inter-Ocean, then a powerful daily and a sort of gospel in the Middle West. He met the 6:30 train every morning, got his supply of newspapers, and had delivered them before he started off for school. At odd times he worked in a gas engine factory. In school he excelled in mathematics. Here he showed the aptitude that subsequently stood him in such good stead in the business world.

Soon after Allyn entered the University of Wisconsin some one told him about the rare opportunity that existed for mining engineers in China. The idea appealed to his imagination for it had the lure of travel to faraway places. Fired with ambition to be a mining engineer he matriculated in the Engineering School.

During his sophomore year Professor Stephen W. Gilman, Professor of Business in the School of Business Administration at the University of Wisconsin, who had become interested in Allyn, said to him:

"Why go to China when you can make money in the United States? You are cut out for a business man. Get engineering out of your system."

So Allyn left the Engineering School and became
a student in the School of Commerce. During school
and vacations he worked for the Wisconsin Tax
Commission where he laid the foundation of practical accounting and finance in which he was to excel.
After graduation, he got a full time job with the Tax
Commission. His first important task for the Commission was to make an audit of Mercer County.
Meanwhile he had secured a position with Price
Waterhouse & Co., the accountants, and was to start
work for them on January 1st, 1914.

Now came one of those curious turns of the wheel
of fate which shape and influence men's lives. Allyn
went to Dayton to attend a wedding. He saw in a
local paper that the NCR welcomed visitors. In
some years 30,000 people visited the plant. It was
part of John H. Patterson's larger publicity scheme.
Allyn visited the factory along with a crowd of pil-
grims. He was not only struck with its efficiency but
was impressed by one particular thing he saw.

In the main hall of the office building was a huge
chart which recounted "82 Reasons why the NCR
Progresses." Fifth among the reasons was "no relatives." In Madison, Allyn had seen industrial plants
and offices cluttered with relations of executives and
large stockholders who held jobs because of their
relationship. The "no relatives" appealed to young
Allyn, for he felt that he would have an opportunity
for advancement in this institution. He went back

home determined to return to Dayton and get a job at NCR.

The realization of Allyn's ambition to work for the NCR was anticipated. Some one had told John H. Patterson that Wisconsin produced a sturdy type of young men. What probably appealed to him more than any other consideration was the fact, as his informant has said, that these Wisconsin lads were not "society boys." Patterson sent F. W. Atkins, who was what Hollywood today would call a "talent scout," out to Madison to prospect. He went to the University of Wisconsin where Allyn was recommended to him.

Late in December 1913 Allyn started in at the NCR. He was 22, lithe, eager, alert. After securing a room at the Y.M.C.A., he took a walk. Compared with the more or less academic aloofness of Madison, the community that was to become his home seemed gay and even alluring. Men with plug hats had been a novelty in Madison. Now he could feast his eyes on many of them.

Allyn was not dismayed when he reported for work the next morning and learned that the hours for work were from 6:30 in the morning until 5:15 in the afternoon. "I am game," he said to himself. He was to prove, once he struck his stride, that like John H. Patterson he, too, was "a little man with a dynamo inside."

The first job assigned to Allyn was as assistant in the Bulletin Room. Patterson's passion for charts, pyramids, and bulletins extended to every angle of the business. In this way Allyn got an early knowledge of company affairs. Within six months business slumped, the factory went on a 3-day work week, and his $20 a week pay was reduced to $12. Soon after this slash in salary Allyn was transferred to the Sales Department. He went out with salesmen; watched them sell, and thus mastered another facet of the business.

Came 1915. The first World War was in full swing. Cash register sales, like those of many other specialties, declined. The Company began to lose money. Patterson asked Price Waterhouse & Co. to make a special investigation of NCR finances. It was placed in charge of W. E. Seatree of the Price Waterhouse staff.

In the meantime Allyn had attracted the attention of John H. Patterson. One day Patterson passed him in the main hall. He was struck with the purposeful way Allyn walked and made inquiry about him saying: "That young man has the most efficient walk I have ever seen." On another occasion Patterson attended a meeting which dealt with financial matters. Allyn was asked to make a chart demonstration. He slammed the figures on the paper in the quick, decisive way that always marks his actions. When he finished Patterson said:

"That's the way I like to see figures presented."

Working with Seatree on the Company audit

Allyn, in the meantime, had demonstrated an unusual ability in accounting. The post of Assistant Comptroller of NCR became vacant and a member of the Price Waterhouse staff was named to fill it.

It was the custom of John H. Patterson to ask a new executive to dine at Far Hills and meet with other company officials. Patterson, therefore, asked the new Assistant Comptroller and a number of other employees including Allyn to dinner. With Patterson the social side was always subordinate to business. His dinners became company forums.

In the midst of the dinner in question Patterson, who was no respecter of appetite, said to the guest of honor:

"Please tell us something about yourself."

The guest got up and began to talk. Suddenly he looked down at his place at the table and said:

"My soup is getting cold."

If he had acquainted himself with any of the basic facts about Patterson he would have known that with this remark he violated one of the major precepts in the Patterson code. He sealed his doom by being more concerned about his soup than his job. As soon as he had given utterance to his solicitude his host said:

"Do not let your soup get cold. By all means eat it at once."

On the following day the position of Assistant Comptroller was vacant. As a matter of fact it was vacant the moment the young man sat down.

Patterson discussed eligibles for the post with Seatree whereupon the latter said:

"You have the ideal man for the job right here in the NCR organization."

"Who is it?" asked Patterson.

"It's young Allyn. Make him Assistant Comptroller and you will never regret it."

Allyn got the job. He was 25 when he put his foot on the first rung of the executive ladder. Within a year he was named Comptroller. In 1918 he was elected director, the youngest man ever to sit on the NCR board. Promotion was now rapid. The year 1926 saw him Treasurer. Four years later he took over the Executive Vice-President's office. The title was subsequently changed to Vice-President and General Manager. In 1940 he became President.

Such is the cycle of self-made success that Allyn has rounded out. His rise has been certain and solid for he is endowed with the qualities out of which industrial chieftainship is wrought. His memory is prodigious. He knows the name of nearly every salesman in the employ of NCR; the facts and figures of the company history and business are at his fingers' ends. He marks the birthday of every fellow executive, Branch Manager, and factory foreman with an individual letter of congratulation. Such acts of this, together with his magnetic personality, bind the NCR family to him. He feels that he owes much to John H. Patterson, whom he greatly admired, so much so that when confronted with a problem he is apt to say to himself:

"What would John H. Patterson do in a situation like this?"

The influence of the founder lingers.

CHAPTER IV

The Cash Register War

THE history of many of the appliances that have benefited mankind is studded with costly litigation. Fulton and his steamboat, McCormick and his harvester, Morse and his telegraph, Howe and his sewing machine, Ide and his cultivator, Bell and his telephone, and the Wright brothers with their aeroplane, all were forced to appeal to the courts to protect the patent rights on the offspring of their brain and hand.

It was inevitable that John H. Patterson and his National cash register, the pioneer in its field, should ride the storm of court contest. No other mechanism, perhaps, figured in such long and bitter litigation. The National cash register paid the price that originality and superiority of product so often exacts and became for years the almost continuous victim of the traditional imitation which is the "sincerest form of flattery." To imitation of form, operation, and service was added infringement of patent.

The injustice involved in the operation of the many infringing companies that sprang up is obvious. From the start Patterson, once he embarked in the business, had backed his faith in the cash register with all he had, not only in terms of money but with untiring effort as well. When he took over control of what became NCR there was no market for the machines. The demand, as I have already pointed out, had to be created, because merchants had no knowledge of the instrument that would become so indispensable to their business. The demand for the National register was built up by educational advertising, practical demonstration, and expert salesmanship. This was only part of the spade work.

The original National cash registers were crude and cumbersome. Their expanding success was achieved through a multitude of improvements. These improvements were not conjured out of the air. They were the result of years of investigation and the expenditure of millions of dollars. Patterson early established an experimental department where new ideas and inventions were studied and tested to emerge ultimately as progressive links in the development of the machine. Then, and throughout the succeeding years, constant change and increasing utility were the keynotes of progress. Every step of the advance was protected by patents.

Another factor entered the picture. The NCR not only owned the fundamental and other patents on successful cash register production but expended large sums in designing and perfecting special machinery for making register parts and supplies. These machines, most of which were patented, reduced manufacturing costs considerably because they did the work faster and more cheaply than could be done otherwise.

By January 1, 1890, six years after Patterson took over, the NCR owned 86 United States patents covering hundreds of devices. Most of the early patents were of vital importance in the making of a dependable cash register. The original and basic Ritty-Birch patents and the Campbell patent which covered an invention by which a spring-propelled drawer could be released automatically and thrown open by pressing down a key, comprised the cornerstone upon which NCR production was reared. I refer to these patents because they figured largely in the years of litigation in which the Company was plunged.

It is interesting to note that John H. Patterson and his brother Frank took an active personal part in the early mechanical development of their product. They appear on the records as the inventors in 22 patents issued between 1885 and 1895. Among other things they cover "five cent devices" which clarified the registering mechanism for the five cent key and its multiples and a color system for special keys and indicators. The most important patent taken out in the Patterson name prevents tampering with the counter because it tells the proprietor if the lid over the adding wheels has been opened. This invention has been in use for years on press-down key National registers.

As most people know, a patent gives the owner
the sole right to make, sell, and use the patented
article and also the right to sue anyone else who
makes, uses, or sells it save with the owner's consent.
Without this right to sue a patent means nothing.
If a company is advised by competent authority that
its patents are being infringed and wishes to maintain and protect them, it notifies the infringer by
mail or publication. This was done in every instance
when registers infringing NCR patents were placed
on the market. If infringing companies failed to
heed these notices the NCR went to the court for
protection.

What may be termed the era of infringement competition began as early as 1888. Between that year
and the mid-nineties, 84 companies were organized
in the United States to produce cash registers. The
great majority followed an identical pattern. They
were started primarily to force NCR into buying
them out because of their nuisance value. The mach-
inations of these concerns resembled the technique
employed in so-called "strike" suits filed in other
days against big corporations, especially railroads,
by individuals who cooked up a grievance and were
willing to settle for comparatively small sums.

Some of the infringing companies varied the procedure. One kind, for example, bought up scattered
patents on adding machines and converted them into cash registers. Another batch of companies tried
to get on the market with a single type of register

which usually infringed some NCR patent. This proved to be highly impractical because Patterson and his associates had learned that no one type of register meets all demands. Hence the vast variety of National machines today. Other cash register concerns started out on financial shoe-strings and fell by the wayside almost before they got started. All infringers had one common objective. It was to capitalize on the good will, integrity of product, and the increasing market established by NCR through years of effort and expense.

How were these companies able to clutter up the cash register field? If you know anything about the industrial history of the eighties and nineties you know why. Those years comprised the period of "cut-throat" competition. Business ethics were far different from those that obtain today. A successful industrial corporation, particularly one with a highly specialized product like the cash register, was regarded as "fair game" by promoters not handicapped by a moral sense. They were out for what they considered was "easy money." The concentration of so many improvements in one line of registers and the reduction of manufacturing costs through the use of specially designed and patented machinery, soon enabled the NCR to offer and publish widely its Great Guaranty "to provide a better cash register at a lower price than any other company." Unable to meet this sweeping challenge many competitors resorted to a campaign of abuse of NCR, its officers, agents, and product. They attempted to enlist public sympathy by posing as struggling concerns crushed by a "vicious octopus." They tried to sell their registers largely by misrepresentation rather than on merit.

Some of the suits entered against infringing companies were settled quickly by injunctions, or because the defendants, realizing that they could not sell their registers if the infringing features were removed, voluntarily went out of business. In other suits progress was slow because appeals were taken to higher courts by the NCR or the defendants. In the meantime infringing companies continued to make and sell registers. Competition naturally became keen.

Thrown on its own resources by reason of the long court delays NCR was compelled to meet the unfair tactics of its competitors as best it could and with everything it had. The majority of the infringing companies, on the other hand, sought desperately to make NCR buy them out, or to force them into other settlements favorable to themselves. In most cases these objectives, let me repeat, represented the sole reasons for their entry into the cash register business.

During the early period of bitter competition the so-called "premium" registers put in their appearance. They were given away or sold at low prices by manufacturers and distributors of cigars, tobacco, liquors, spices, and chewing gum with orders for their merchandise. They were cheap, flimsy, undependable, and therefore unable to meet competition with NCR. Because of the impracticability of their registers or lack of capital, nine companies making premium registers discontinued business but not until one of them contributed a degree of humor to the embattled situation.

In 1894 a Detroit cafe owner, Michael Heintz by name, organized the Heintz Cash Register Co. with a capital stock of $10,000. The company started to make a register called "Cuckoo" which was sold for $85. Instead of ringing a bell with each operation of the machine a bird would emerge from an arrangement similar to that on a cuckoo clock and make a sound resembling "cuckoo." The NCR filed suit against Heintz in August 1895 for infringement of the Campbell cash drawer patent and secured a permanent injunction which silenced the cuckoo. An accounting for profits and damages was waived because Heintz had manufactured and sold only a few machines.

A more pretentious premium register enterprise was launched by the Ideal Cash Register Company, incorporated September 30, 1897 at Bound Brook, New Jersey, and capitalized at $1,000,000. This company was organized to manufacture a line of lever-set, crank-operated registers to be sold with medicines which were nationally advertised. None of the Ideal machines was sold until nearly three years after incorporation.

The campaign of the Ideal Cash Register Company was so typical of the methods employed against NCR that they are well worth relating in detail. Several months before their registers were ready for the market the company printed in its house organ, "Every Now and Then," which was widely distributed among the drug trade, a thinly veiled attack on the NCR product stating that it was cheaply made, inaccurate, cumbersome, out of date, and top priced.

The Ideal Company now came out in the open for the first of a long line of denunciations. In their first catalogue and price list they ridiculed and attacked NCR machines stating that the detail strip, check printer, and other special attachments on National registers were "ornamental jim-cracks which cumber the machine and add little to its value but serve as an excuse for exorbitant prices." In the following year Ideal printed and distributed a circular headed "Fourteen ways of beating the National cash register -79, one of their latest highest priced registers." Then followed 14 questions and answers as to how this register could be manipulated so as to prove inaccurate.

The NCR filed suit against the Ideal Company on July 3, 1902 for infringement of the Cleal patent covering the automatic return of all adding segments to zero after each operation. A fortnight later a second suit was filed under another Cleal patent protecting indicating mechanism.

Every key in the scale of abuse was played by the

Ideal Company. Its campaign of villification, however, netted nothing. The concern encountered great
difficulty in selling its product. In order to get their
registers on the market Ideal offered them as pre-
miums at a discount of 50 per cent with orders for
$50 worth of medicines. This proposal failed be-
cause merchants had come to realize the value of
features and attachments on National machines and
were willing to pay the difference in price to get
them. When the Ideal Company did put out a register with a detail strip and a check printer at an
increased price it was unable to regain the ground
lost. Business slumped. The factory was closed down
in 1903. In April 1904 the corporation went into
the hands of a receiver. Thus ended a chapter in the
long and troubled story of NCR patent litigation.

All this litigation, which formed only part of the
battle waged against NCR by infringing companies,
was the prelude to a larger court drama which drew
the national spotlight. It began in the early nineties
when Henry S. Hallwood, then engaged in the street
paving block business in Columbus, Ohio, bought
the Sern P. Watt patents on a drawer-operated cash
register and organized the Hallwood Cash Register
Company to manufacture Hallwood registers. Hallwood's object in forming the Company, as revealed
in an affidavit, was to make a speculation out of the
business and force the NCR to buy him out once he
launched his enterprise.

In March 1897 NCR sued the Hallwood Com-

pany for infringement of the Maxwell Patent which
protected a device that locked all the keys on a register while the drawer was open. A similar suit was
entered against the New Columbus Watch Company
as manufacturers of the infringing machines. The
Hallwood Company now sued NCR for $100,000
damages alleging unfair competition and conspiracy
to restrain trade. With these suits began the bitter
legal controversy that continued for 18 years and
eventually led to Federal intervention. Suits and
counter suits followed thick and fast.

The Hallwood Company became financially involved and went out of business. Hallwood retained
the patents under which his original company had
operated and formed the International Register
Company. This, in turn, was succeeded by several
other corporations. Out of the conglomeration of
companies finally emerged the American Cash Register Company which obtained the rights to the Hallwood patents. The NCR then sued the American
for infringements of one of its patents. Once more
litigation flared.

Finding that their tactics had caused the NCR no
more serious trouble than a vast amount of effort,
annoyance, and expense, the American Company
now decided to strike through the Federal Government. Representatives of the American appeared before the Department of Justice at Washington in
1910 and filed complaint against NCR.

Federal agents combed the entire country and

thirty years of NCR history for evidence which the
government might use in its prosecution. The point
to be emphasized is that the Government, in building up its case, resurrected the past and adapted it
to what was then the present. During the years of
bitter infringement litigation NCR, as I have said,
had to fight with everything it had to protect its
legal rights. These rights had been amply vindicated
in the courts. In an era of "cut-throat" competition
it had fought fire with fire.

In addition to the criminal action a civil suit was
filed against NCR by United States Attorney General Wickersham in December 1911 in the United
States District Court for Southern Ohio at Cincinnati. His petition was based largely on the charge
of conspiracy to restrain trade.

In its February 1912 term the United States Grand
Jury for the District Court of Southern Ohio, at
the instance of District Attorney Sherman T. Mc-
Pherson, handed down an indictment against John
H. Patterson and 21 other NCR officials charging
them with criminal conspiracy under the Sherman
Anti-Trust Law. The indictment contained three
counts: (1) conspiracy to restrain trade and create
a monopoly; (2) unlawfully monopolizing the trade
in cash registers; (3) continuing to hold and carry
on the business so built up.

The American Cash Register Company could not
have chosen a more propitious time to instigate the
prosecution of the NCR. The wave of heckling and

harrying of so-called "big business," was at its height. In a considerable section of the popular mind the name of a "captain of industry" had become anathema. It was not difficult, therefore, to secure an indictment against anything or anybody that represented what the rabble-rousers called "predatory capital." The NCR was a victim of the spirit of the times.

When NCR filed a demurrer to the indictment on the ground that the counts were uncertain and defective the court overruled it. Thereupon NCR entered a plea of "not guilty." A jury was impanelled and the trial began November 20th, 1912.

The Government contended that NCR was doing 95 per cent of all cash register business and sought to impress the jury that this, in itself constituted a monopoly. When counsel for NCR tried to introduce evidence that whatever of a so-called monopoly it held was the natural and lawful result of basic patents, a liberal research and experimental policy, a superior product, and a large and efficient manufacturing and selling organization, the court refused to admit it. Throughout the entire course of the trial the NCR was unable to present to the jury any part of the mass of evidence concerning its patent rights, their infringement, and the vicious competition it had been compelled to meet. Practically all the evidence submitted by the Government related to incidents that had occurred many years before when fierce competition in business was the common procedure.

Despite the combing of the whole country by Government agents, assisted by hostile competitors of the National Company, the Government was able to present only 32 cases of alleged interference with competitors' sales by NCR agents. Of these only three were proved by the evidence introduced. Records showed that in the three years immediately preceding the indictment the 1,000 agents and salesmen of the NCR made 3,000,000 calls on merchants. This meant that approximately one call in each million was proved to be an interference with a competitor's business.

On February 13, 1913 the jury returned a verdict of "guilty" on each count of the indictment. The court then imposed a fine of $5,000, payment of costs, and the sentence of a year in jail on Patterson. Sentences ranging from payment of costs and nine months or a year in jail was given to the other defendants. The defendants immediately filed notice of intention to apply for a writ of error and were granted four months in which to prepare and file a bill of exceptions.

In this dark hour Nature took a hand by projecting Patterson into a conspicuous public service. Less than five weeks after he had been sentenced, the Dayton flood broke. I have already told how Patterson's genius for organization converted the NCR plant into a haven of refuge and relief for the flood victims. Overnight he became a national figure. While the dirt and debris still choked the Dayton streets hundreds of well meaning persons sent messages to President Wilson urging him to pardon Patterson in recognition of his great humanitarian work during the flood. As soon as he heard of this activity the head of the NCR sent the following characteristic telegram to the President:

"Our case is still in the courts. I do not ask for, nor would I accept, a pardon. All I want is simple justice."

After the bill of exceptions had been made part of the record of the case, counsel for NCR argued their brief in the United States Court of Appeals beginning October 6, 1914. The Court consisted of Justice William Day of the Supreme Court of the United States, and District Judges Cochran of Kentucky and Sanford of Tennessee. Their decision was read by Judge Cochran on March 13, 1915.

The decision held that both the second and third counts of the indictment were defective because of uncertainty and duplicity and that the trial court had erred in overruling the defendants' demurrer to them. It held further that the sole issue in the first count was whether NCR had conspired, in the manner charged, against the American Company within the three years immediately preceding the indictment. A further ruling was that the defendants were entitled to show the competitive tactics of American in order that the jury might determine whether there was a conspiracy in restraint of trade, or whether the alleged acts were to be accounted for by reason of the aggressions and unfair competition of the American Company.

The Court also held that while the Government evidence regarding NCR's activities in the old days was admissible, the trial court had further erred in refusing to admit evidence offered by the National Company to show that most of the competitors were infringers of their patents and that such of the conduct complained of as a conspiracy in restraint of trade was only the natural result of these provocations and aggressions by competitors. Evidence of this nature had been practically the sole defense of NCR and its officials. The refusal of the trial court to admit it had virtually thrown them upon the mercy of a jury that had heard only one side of the story.

For the reasons just stated the Court of Appeals reversed the judgment of the trial court and remanded the case back for a new trial to conform with its decisions.

It so happened that I sat alongside John H. Patterson on that fateful March morning in 1915. He had asked me to be with him on a day that would spell triumph or disaster for him. He sat unperturbed during the reading of the 57 page decision. When Judge Cochran uttered the words: "We are constrained, therefore, to reverse the judgment of the lower court," he did not show a trace of emotion then, or when his fellow defendants and many friends crowded around to offer congratulations.

Patterson and his party arrived in Dayton early in the evening of the memorable day. His homecoming was marked by a demonstration without precedent in the city's history. A parade was formed with the President of the NCR at the head. Twenty thousand persons marched in the procession and many more watched from roofs, windows, and sidewalks. Flags waved, red fire flared, bands played, and the people cheered. All classes joined in the tribute to the community's foremost citizen.

Deeply touched by the outpouring of his fellow towns-people Patterson issued this message:

"To My Friends, Neighbors, and Fellow-Workers of Dayton:

"On behalf of myself, and twenty-one colleagues who have been associated with me during the last two years of strenuous times, I want to thank you for this splendid welcome. I have had many home-comings, but none in my life has been equal to this indorsement of the decision of the Court of Appeals at which we were present in Cincinnati today. That decision means not only much to our industry but to all other industries of the United States.

"I am thankful and grateful for the decision of the Court of Appeals. It was, however, what we had a right to expect from three just and able men. Much as I value it, I value this indorsement of that decision by the court of my home people where I was born and where I have lived all my life.

"I hope that this means a new era of prosperity, not

only for our city but for our country. I hope it will
enable the officers and people of our company to concentrate on making our chimneys smoke six days a week
instead of three days.

"Words feebly express my thanks to each one of you
for this great demonstration. Remarks of approval
are always grateful, but when they are re-enforced by
good wishes and confidence, they are doubly grateful."

Attorney General Wickersham and District Attorney McPherson now sought to take the case to
the Supreme Court of the United States on a writ
of certiorari. On June 14, 1915 the highest court in
the land refused to entertain the motion, thus making
the Circuit Court of Appeals reversal of the trial
Court's judgment final.

The decision of the Supreme Court did not ter-
minate the action against Patterson and his associates.
The first count of the original indictment, with the
modifications and restrictions imposed by the Court
of Appeals, still held. The civil suits were pending.
The defendants could have stood re-trial with a
reasonable expectation of acquittal in view of the
Court of Appeals ruling on the evidence as well as
the form of the indictment itself. A long trial would
have meant the expenditure of a tremendous amount
of money and taken company officials away from
business for months. In view of this situation, counsel
for the Government and the defendants agreed upon
the entry of a *nolle prosequi* in the criminal case and
a consent decree in the civil case.

CHAPTER V

Salesmen Are Made

DURING his long and busy life the name of John H. Patterson became synonymous with many pioneer industrial procedures. They were labelled impractical, even visionary at the start. Today all are incorporated into successful management. Among the many NCR "firsts" that he initiated are welfare for workers, the factory suggestion system, daylight factories, factory medical care with clinics and visiting nurses, health education, foremen's meetings, the house organ, motion pictures in industry, dining rooms and noon-day entertainment for employees, industrial and community relations, rest periods and rest rooms for women workers, and night schools for the further training and education of ambitious employees.

To no branch of modern business, however, did Patterson make a more significant contribution than to salesmanship where he recorded another historic "first." He found it a more or less haphazard vocation; he made of it a science to be studied just as the law, medicine, or engineering are studied. He established the first sales school and with it brought dignity and distinction to selling.

It was characteristic of Patterson to fly in the face of tradition. His refusal to accept the established order, whether in production or distribution, if there was any possibility of improving upon it, made him an insurgent but always the far-seeing and constructive rebel. For years the saying: "Salesman are born not made," ruled American selling. Patterson thought otherwise. He felt that salesmen could be made. With firm faith in this idea he inaugurated the training of salesmen. From a group of five agents gathered in a room in a downtown Dayton hotel developed the technique and curriculum of a University of Business that has launched thousands of men on worthwhile careers.

The sales school and all that it implies sprang from one of the passions of Patterson's life. Education, as you have already seen, was his fetich. He, himself, was always avid for information. Shakespeare said that "all the world's a stage." The founder of the NCR believed that all the world's a school.

To understand the inspiration of the first NCR sales school it is necessary to get a bird's-eye view of American business back to the eighties. The history of our economic development indicates that there was no vital need for trained salesmen prior to the time of Patterson's acquisition of what became the NCR. Up to that period markets expanded more rapidly than production. The demand for most goods exceeded the supply. In other words, merchandise was practically self-selling.

The beginning of the age of mechanization altered the picture. Projection of machines as an aid to business, especially retailing, struck at the basic reluctance of human nature to accept change. Patterson's cash register was an innovation. It stood in the van of the mechanization that was to work miracles of efficiency and service. Few people, however, had heard of the cash register. Patterson's first problem, therefore, was to educate the merchant to the need of his product. Since education was one of his passions, he became the happy warrior battling on a favorite field.

Obviously if Patterson was to educate the merchants to use cash registers, he had first to train salesmen for the task. At once he ran afoul a fixed habit. As production in the United States caught up with demand, competitive selling got under way with a technique that Patterson was destined to doom. The early NCR salesmen, determined to get orders despite all obstacles, often out-talked the prospect. They used the sheer weight of personality and an avalanche of words to get their product over. This high pressure selling, with the accent on personality, largely inspired the widely held belief that "salesmen are born."

Patterson held that while the power of personality as a force in selling is undeniable, it is just one factor in the performance. In the Patterson lexicon it had to be re-enforced by knowledge of what is being sold, as well as knowledge of the needs and requirements of the potential user. He felt that sales could be consummated not so much by aggressive methods as by the logical influencing of the customer into admitting that he needed a cash register and the service it offered.

There was ample provocation for the high-pressure formula back in those early selling days. The business of selling was as lusty as the times in which the hammer and tongs methods were employed. There was a reason. The cash register protected the merchant from dishonesty and the clerk from temptation. The salesman was up against a double-barrelled obstacle because the retailer was instinctively opposed to change, and the clerk resented intrusion upon what he regarded as his pilfering prerogative. The cash register, therefore, called for strong selling because of the stout sales resistance it encountered.

Through this period of trial and error evolved the basis of all creative selling thereafter. It meant that it was first necessary to sell the prospect on the idea that his store system was important and that his profits were affected by it, that the system should be diagnosed as to its soundness or weakness and, what was equally important, that the NCR salesman was qualified to assist in the investigation. Animating all this was an old NCR slogan: "There is in every store a need which, when uncovered, will lead to the sale of a National cash register."

It is a curious fact that while John H. Patterson was in no sense a salesman, he had an uncanny understanding of the elements that are comprised in selling. His inquiring mind began to probe more and more into the methods employed by his salesmen. Whenever one of the agents came to Dayton from the field Patterson's invariable first question was, "How do you sell cash registers?"

One day in 1886 he got five full time agents, at that time NCR machines were sometimes sold as a side line, to meet with him in a room in the Phillips House. After propounding his usual first question to each of them he started what became a little forum in selling. It was, in all likelihood, the first sales conference ever held in this country.

The ace salesman of those pioneer NCR days was Joseph H. Crane. In a preceding chapter I have told how Patterson secured a verbatim account of his selling talk and had the typed copy of it brought out in a little pamphlet called "The Primer" which the agents were required to memorize. This paper-back pamphlet was the first sales manual, fore-runner of the vast amount of selling literature with which every salesman is now familiar. "The Primer" was succeeded by other selling books each one more detailed than its predecessor culminating in the impressive Sales Manuals of today.

The deeper Patterson delved into the selling

methods of his agents the more he realized that high-pressure tactics were unsatisfactory. He found that prospects resented the strenuous approach and objected to being browbeaten into submission to a sale. To be sure, the high-pressure process brought in business. The head of the NCR maintained, however, that there was another and better way to equip the agent for the selling campaign. Again the Patterson interest in education asserted itself, this time to effect a memorable innovation that established still another mile-post in NCR history and influenced all selling.

From time to time Patterson visited agents in the field and called them together for sales conferences in Dayton. He presided over these gatherings like a school master. He did a better job here than in his immediate post-college days when he taught school for a brief period. That proved to be an uncongenial task. The flair for teaching, however, was innate. It manifested itself effectively when he applied himself to a subject that was dear to his heart. This was his own business.

After Patterson had canvassed all his agents he said:

"If the agents can sell registers by their present methods, they can certainly sell twice as many as if they are carefully trained to employ improved methods."

On April 4, 1894 Patterson opened the first sales agents training school in the United States. The school house was a small structure located near the NCR factory and came to be known as "the cottage under the elm." The teacher was Joseph H. Crane.

Once the school was established Patterson decreed that all NCR agents must take the course. The company paid the transportation and hotel bills of the students and gave then $3 a week for pocket money. The initial class numbered 37 men. The first textbook was "The Primer." The booklet was changed so many times that students entered a complaint on the ground that no sooner did they learn one version of "The Primer" than it was changed. Patterson then engaged a Harvard professor to convert "The Primer" material into a standard manual.

Study of "The Primer" and its successors comprised only part of the school course. Patterson's passion for wider education was now unleashed. The students were taught to demonstrate all the National registers then being produced. They also studied price lists, store methods, and the technique of retailing. To give a touch of realism Patterson had model grocery and drug stores and butcher shops built with dummy merchandise. This gave the students a store atmosphere for their training.

Patterson would never permit a sales student to learn how to repair a register. He even prohibited the men from carrying screw-drivers. He based his objection on the belief, as he once expressed it, that "a mechanically-minded agent with a screw-driver would spend so much time tinkering with a machine

that he might forget to sell one." This implied no
disregard of knowledge of the mechanical structure
of the register. Familiarity with all its details was
a "must" feature of the training. Out of the feeling
that sales and repairs be divorced, emerged the Repair School of Dayton.

Another basic principle established in the early
sales training day was that all instructors must be
salesmen. There was no academic theorizing in the
NCR curriculum then or now. Men who know how
to sell teach how to sell. They capitalize their knowledge and practical experience for the benefit of the
classes.

Patterson impressed upon all sales students, as well
as on salesmen the importance of a neat appearance.
Often, as I have already related, he provided agents
with complete wardrobes at his own expense. He felt
strongly that the successful agent must "sell" himself
first. One of his admonitions was: "Always conduct
yourself in a manner that will reflect credit on your
company. The company you represent and the product you sell, are judged to a large extent by your
actions."

Soon after the opening of the Sales School it
became evident that the size of the class —37 men
—operated against complete participation in the
program. The number of students was reduced to
fifteen, the agents coming to Dayton in relays. Patterson then discovered that some students merely
took the course "for the ride" and then went their

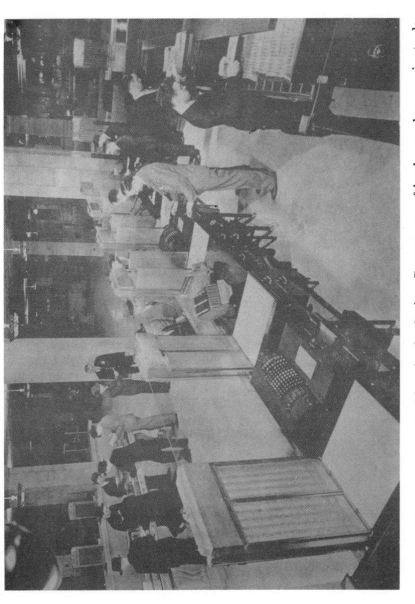

National Window-Posting Machines in the Savings Department of banks speed up service to depositors and eliminate "after-hour" bookkeeping

National Cash Registers mechanically add each item purchased and issue an itemized and totalled receipt for the customer

Each step in machining and assembling has been carefully studied to provide a Departmental layout that enables parts to flow through the department with the minimum amount of handling

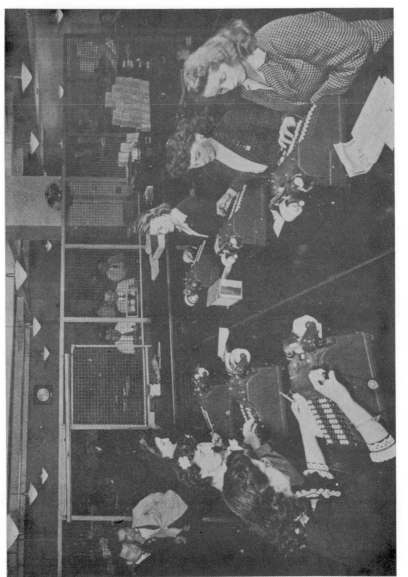

Everywhere the Allen Wales adding machine proves its usefulness

Sugar Camp from the air

A class in session at Sugar Camp

Super market customers appreciate the speed and accuracy in which transactions can be recorded on receipt-printing National Cash Registers, especially designed for check-out stores

National Payroll Machines speed the handling of payroll and writing of checks; this is an installation in a large factory

One type of NCR advertising—folders, booklets, catalogue sheets

way equipped with a basic sales education that did not benefit the company. This led to the rule that a man must spend at least six months in the field before qualifying as a student.

During the first period of the Sales School only NCR salesmen were enrolled. Patterson now conceived the idea of enlisting young men without selling experience who could be moulded into salesmen. His judgment had been amply vindicated as the long line of successful NCR salesmen, some of them Branch Managers, and all Sales School graduates, attests.

Still another mandate, laid down when "the cottage under the elm" was in its infancy holds. It is that an NCR salesman never graduates any more than a doctor, a lawyer, or an engineer ever reaches the point where he need no longer study. This is peculiarly applicable to the NCR product. If it remained static, so to speak, there would be no need of continuous study. The product, however, is subject to constant change and improvement. Moreover, new applications are being continually found for machines in use. The salesman must keep pace with all this change. Hence the evolution of sales training parallels the evolution of what the NCR produces. Every assemblage of NCR agents, whether in the Hundred Point Conventions, District meetings, or conferences at the Dayton factory, become informal post-graduate courses.

The evolution of the NCR product provides only

one reason why sales training must be fluid and constant. Salesmen are trained in the trends of merchandising. When the National cash register first went on the market it met a simple need which was to protect cash in a store. The majority of American stores then were small with a few clerks selling limited lines of goods for cash only. As the shops grew in size, expanded their lines, and began to sell on credit, National machines were developed to meet the new needs. It followed that methods of selling became more complicated. It was increasingly important, therefore, that NCR salesmen know all there was to know about merchandising, store lay-out, and bookkeeping. By this time the successful operation of a store demanded a National register. It was up to the salesman to widen its applications to meet the changes in merchandising methods. The Sales School equips him for this work.

One scorching day in the summer of 1903, Patterson visited the Sales School. He found the students sweltering in the humid heat. The class room was a hot box. Realizing that the men could not concentrate on their studies amid such discomfort he decided to do something about it. On the following morning when he was taking his daily horseback ride accompanied by a company executive, he pulled up on a tree-studded hill which overlooked the factory and the city of Dayton. As he surveyed the lovely sylvan scene he said to his companion:

"This is the site for the Sales School. We will move in here at once."

When Patterson decided to do something he did it fast. There was no time to erect buildings so Patterson did the next best thing. Within forty-eight hours a tent city gleamed amid the maples and the elms on that hill top. Thus rose what came to be known as the University under Canvas.

Capacity enrollment became the rule. In 1931, for example, 269 students were registered. They came from 41 States and two Canadian Provinces. The average age of the men was 30 years. More than a hundred sales agencies were represented. The size of this class and its wide geographical distribution was typical of all subsequent sessions.

The Sales School remained under canvas until 1934 when permanent buildings were erected on the site. The tree-embowered hill had once been a maple sugar camp. John H. Patterson had collected sugar water there in his boyhood days. The School, therefore, became Sugar Camp, alma mater for thousands of young men who have embarked on successful selling careers from its campus. Sugar Camp has become the symbol of NCR training. It is known not only throughout the worldwide NCR organization, but is regarded as a model wherever salesmanship is studied. Nearly every important industrial concern that markets its product through a sales organization now has a Sales School. The cottage under the elm pointed the way.

The Sugar Camp program comprises a complete business college course. Here ambitious young men are educated to be counsellors in merchandising and accounting administration. Here salesmanship is elevated to the dignity of a profession.

The Sugar Camp plant represents a capital investment of over a half million dollars and costs many thousands for yearly maintenance and operation. The NCR pays all expenses as well as salaries to the students while they study or are training in the field. There are 60 four-man cabins, six air-conditioned class rooms, an air-conditioned assembly hall seating 320 persons, administration building, recreation and dining halls and campus. Ample diversions are provided by a swimming pool, shuffle board, badminton and tennis courts and a soft ball diamond. During the Second World War Sugar Camp was occupied by the WAVES.

While Sugar Camp and the Sales Manuals provide the major part of the training of salesmen other factors are projected into the course. One of the most constructive and important of these supplementary aids is the consulting relationship between branch managers, territory managers, and senior salesmen, and the junior salesmen and trainees. Men in supervisory capacities have found that it is good business to pass on their "know how" to those around them and especially to beginners in the field. The result is a camaraderie that makes for close working kinship.

This "personalized" training, as it is called, means that some sales executive or senior salesman sits down and talks across the desk with a junior salesman, finding out in this informal way the things that may be troubling him, and giving him the answers of experience. It may also mean that they will accompany each other on visits to users or prospects. Such procedure helps to develop confidence and a pattern of thinking that enables the junior member to meet difficult situations when they arise once he is on his own.

When the NCR entered upon the production of accounting machines in 1921 a new vista of sales training opened up. Prior to this time people referred to the National industry as a "specialty" business. This was now out of date. The NCR became designers, manufacturers, and distributors of business machines while the sales organization emerged as a small army of system engineers.

Adoption of National accounting machines was a natural evolution because the mechanized way had demonstrated its superiority. Preference for NCR mechanized systems to old-fashioned and out-moded hand methods was as logical as man's preference for an electric refrigerator to an ice box, an automobile to a horse and buggy, a motion picture to a magic lantern show. The complexities of construction, plus the great variety of uses of accounting machines, made special qualifications for salesmen necessary. To basic knowledge of retailing and bookkeeping was now added specialized knowledge of business administration, office methods and procedures whether in banking or industry, as well as all phases of accounting in stores. The curriculum of the Sales School was therefore expanded to include these fields.

At first the accounting machine salesmen were drawn principally from the cash register selling force. These pioneers in what was then a virgin field for NCR were soon augmented by specialists from business, finance, and industry who knew accounting needs and practices. As soon as their specialized knowledge was adapted to NCR selling, it was passed on to the men already selling accounting machines and to the new salesmen recruited for the work. Here you have another example of the evolution in training and selling as it kept pace with the development of the product. By this process of education NCR salesmen became sales engineers functioning as consultants to industry, banking, public utilities, railroads, hotels, and business generally.

To provide the basis of accounting machine training a Sales Reference Library has been developed through the years. It consists of thirteen volumes, each one a Sales Manual, which comprises the text books for Sugar Camp and offer, in their entirety, a liberal education in business, accounting procedure, and selling. Truly a "Five Foot Book Shelf" of salesmanship.

Before the trainee reaches the Reference Library stage he must study sections of the Sales Manual devoted to the evolution of the cash register, qualifications for NCR salesmen, and a chapter entitled "How to Study." The first lap on the road to Sugar Camp is mastery of the Field Training Course, which constitutes the preparatory school in the salesman's education. This course of study provides a consistent, basic training plan for every accounting machine salesman regardless of the size of the branch office that may employ him. It must be completed before he is accepted in the Sales School. The completion of the plan assures trainees that all enter the school with the same knowledge.

The trainee is obliged to spend sixteen weeks in the field while studying the Field Training Course. He receives pay from the day he starts this course. Thus he earns and learns all the way up from novice to trained salesman. During his Field Training he has contact with branch office operation, watches agents demonstrate and sell machines, makes installations and sometimes accompanies them on their calls. Thus he gets his first conception of actual salesmanship. It is worth noting, in this connection, that twenty per cent of the sales training is by text. The rest is through practical education.

The Field Training Course text book is prepared in loose-leaf form so that trainees can be given a complete assignment, that is, a series of questions for a definite period without anticipating or working on a future assignment. At the end of each assignment the trainee takes a written test which is sent to the Sales Training Department in Dayton together with a progress report from his supervisor. From these reports and tests the Sales Training Department keeps in touch with the status of each aspiring salesman until he is qualified to enter the Sales School. The trainee must then pass a rigid examination on the complete Field Training Course.

With all this study behind him, the trainee is enrolled at Sugar Camp. Here he puts in five intensive weeks using the Reference Library volumes as text books. He is given practical demonstrations of NCR machines by experienced instructors who are all crack salesmen. He tours the factory and sees how the product that he will sell is made. Through contact with the NCR family he catches the spirit that animates the entire organization.

At Sugar Camp the student comes under the ministrations of a faculty composed of masters of their calling. From the day of Joseph H. Crane down to the present time, the instructors and sales training executives have been chosen from men with high selling records and the additional but vitally important qualification of being able to impart what they know to others. Some of the top executives and managers of the larger NCR branches have been teachers in the Sales School.

When the graduate leaves Sugar Camp he is told that his training has just begun. He returns to the branch office and resumes his trips with agents assisting them in making installations and sometimes installing machines himself. After a year or longer, he is invested with the responsibility of salesman and forges forth on his own. There is an NCR tradition that it requires five years for a man to become a full fledged salesman. Ready adaptability frequently shortens this period.

Study does not end with the traditional five year period. Graduates come back to Sugar Camp from time to time for refresher courses and for specific training when new merchandising trends develop. A new trend developed with the shift in food stores from clerk service to check-out or self service. The NCR had a machine, the 6000—otherwise known as the Itemizer—to meet this need. Every NCR cash register salesman was trained in this innovation and how to assist food merchants in the change-over to the new store operation. Another instance of the need of new specialized instruction followed the introduction of the improved payroll machine. All accounting machine salesmen were trained in the specific problems that apply to payroll writing.

Periodical reunions of what in college parlance are called "old grads" at Sugar Camp are invariably converted into informal sales schools. The men, all veterans in their lines, gather in genial fellowship to talk shop. They discuss new accounting problems, and review and revise old ones. They exchange ideas, acquire new knowledge, and return to their territories better equipped for their jobs. These reunions and their practical by-products emphasize anew the fact that an NCR salesman never graduates.

How are the students for Sugar Camp recruited? There are various sources from which the men needed for the selling organization are drawn. College graduating classes provide one. The NCR salesmen in the field find desirable material in banks, industries, and businesses when they contact users or prospects. A bank official, for example, will say to a National representative:

"John Smith over there is a capable young man but he dislikes confinement in a counting room all day. He has an agreeable way with people, considerable personality, and would like a more active life. He would be happier as a salesman." So John Smith becomes a candidate for the NCR Sales School. Frequently men employed in businesses that use NCR products become so interested in the machines that they want to have a part in selling them. Finally, there is the type of young man who has heard or read so much about the NCR and its methods that he feels that there is a future for him with the company.

There is food for thought and a stimulus for action in a book called "Your 100,000 Hours" issued by the NCR Sales Training Department. The title is derived from the following statement in the book:

"A young man at the age of 25 years has about 100,000 working hours before he reaches the retirement age. How he should invest these 100,000 hours as to the choice of company, its product and policies, is his Number One job."

This statement has peculiar significance at a time of drastic human adjustment and readjustment without precedent in history. Many men must seek new vocations. To a greater degree, perhaps, than ever before scientific salesmanship offers the opportunity for a constructive and profitable career. On this score the book, "Your 100,000 Hours," says:

"Selling is as basic as manufacturing because it is the distribution source to a world of need. Selling not only has thrill and adventure but is a form of public service. The salesman is a benefactor of society. Scientific development for the benefit of humanity begins in the laboratory but it requires the salesman to make this development available to the public. There is always a good income for a successful salesman. The best paid people in most organizations are the salesmen. Many important executives come up through the sales route."

In this connection it is interesting to point to the imposing list of high-placed business executives and other leaders who had much or all of their training at the NCR. Among the distinguished alumni of the Company are: Willian E. Best, Works Manager, Remington Arms Company; I. S. Betts, Vice President, Remington Arms Company; William F. Bockhoff, President, National Automatic Tool Company; Hugh Chalmers, who was President of the Chalmers Motor Car Company; William A. Chryst, Chief

Engineer, Delco; Frank O. Clements, Director of
Research, General Motors Research Corporation;
Frank Parker Davis of Davis, Lindsey, Smith and
Shonts, Chicago; H. F. Devens, New York; Frank
L. Ditzler, Western Zone Manager, Toledo Scale
Company; Herbert G. Dorsey, Principal Electrical
Engineer, Chief Research Section, United States
Coast and Geodetic Survey; Joseph E. Fields, Vice
President, Chrysler Corporation; R. H. Grant, Vice
President, General Motors Corporation; John B.
Hayward, International Business Machines Cor-
poration; Edward S. Jordan, President, Jordan
Motor Car Company; C. F. Kettering, President
Research Laboratories Division, General Motors
Corporation; A. J. Lauver, General Manager, Bur-
roughs Adding Machine Company; William A.
LeBrun, Foreign Agent, Toleda Scale Company;
Alvan Macauley, Chairman, Packard Motor Car
Company; Joseph McAdams, President, Steel Prod-
ucts Engineering Company; Lester F. Mitchell,
Manager of Engineering, Addressograph-Multi-
graph Corporation; E. C. Morse, President Export
Division, Chrysler Corporation; Fred W. Nichol,
Vice President and General Manager, International
Business Machines Corporation; Earl L. Reeder,
President, Dayton Coca-Cola Bottling Company;
Joseph E. Rogers, President, Addressograph-Multi-
graph Corporation; William Sherman, President,
Standard Register Company; Henry Theobald,
President, Toledo Scale Company; H. E. Wall of

Wall, Cassell and Groneweg, Dayton; Thomas J. Watson, President, International Business Machines Corporation; Samuel H. West, Judge United States District Court, Sixth Circuit, Ohio; Wendell E. Whipp, President, Monarch Machine Tool Company.

All the schooling at NCR is not confined to the training of salesmen. There is also a school for repair men. Service, in its broadest sense, requires meeting not only all user needs through efficient operation of machines but keeping the machines in constant good repair as well. Men must be trained for this work. The NCR Repair School fits them for the job.

Once more you have a highly organized training set-up. The Repair School is located on the fifth floor of Building One, an enlargement of the first factory built on the Patterson farm site. Formerly all the students worked in one large room. In 1945 an important change in the training set-up was made. Separate class rooms, each one accommodating ten men, are now provided. Each room is shaped like a horseshoe, open at the end. It is equipped with a blackboard, a projecting screen, and work benches. As a result lectures and work can go on in the same location. Instead of training 70 men a year, the new system enables 210 to be trained every twelve months. Up to January 1st, 1945, 3,114 students have graduated from the Repair School. Experienced repair men are the instructors.

The NCR Repair School capitalizes the significant changes made in the industrial training of men due to the pressure of war work especially in the Army and Navy. To get a first hand knowledge of these changes William J. Schaefer, Head of the Repair School, visited Army and Navy Training Depots, editors of training magazines, producers of training films, and private industries.

Just as the embryo salesman does his stint at a branch office before going to Sugar Camp, so does the apprentice for the Repair School spend six months in the repair shop of a branch office. Here his aptitude is appraised. Once he meets the test he is enrolled in the Repair School where he remains for 25 weeks. In addition to the technical side of the training, the student goes through commercial courses and studies employee-customer relations and also company-employee relations. Educational films and lectures help to steer student thinking into useful channels. The school trains minds as well as hands.

One reason for this diversified training is the opportunity for advancement that the repair job holds out. After installation of a machine the repair man becomes, in many instances, the only link between the user and the Company. His personal appearance, manners, and efficiency are not only important assets for his employer but also contribute to his promotion. Scores of repair men have risen to be salesmen, branch managers, and even to higher stations.

A conspicuous example is Ewing Stumm who started in the repair shop of the Kansas City branch office. Today he is Special Assistant to the Vice-President In Charge Of Sales and supervises sales training. George F. Rogers, Branch Manager at Detroit, and Harry L. Kuykendall, who was Chicago Branch Manager at the time of his death, were students in the Repair School in Dayton.

Improvement in repair equipment keeps abreast with improvement in machines Formerly a group of repair men worked at a long bench. It was usually littered up with material and tools. Furthermore, conversation between the men working close together often impeded work. Perry V. Shoe, Manager of the Overseas Service and Supply, devised an individual work bench with a smooth bowling-alley like top which can easily be kept clean and orderly. These individual units discourage useless conversation between workers. Each man has his own little bailiwick of labor. Another improvement which provides pleasing environment for work is the standardized repair shop in the various branch and other offices.

As is the case with the Sales School, students for the Repair School are obtained in a variety of ways. Some apply for the training because they have heard that it is thorough and offers opportunity for promotion. Others answer NCR advertisements for recruits which appear periodically in newspapers all over the country. Preference is always given the men coming out of the armed services. All repair students receive pay from the day they start in at the branch office.

With sales training, as with repair training and in every other branch of the business, education is constantly on the march at NCR.

CHAPTER VI

The Strategy of Selling

WHEN a man has a physical check-up he frequently finds, much to his surprise, that he has some defect whether in his heart, lungs, kidneys, or elsewhere. Often, in his astonishment, he exclaims: "Why I have never been ill in my life!" He is only superficially well. The same applies to a business. A store may seem to be prospering yet hidden weaknesses sap profit and undermine its health. Every business, therefore, needs a diagnostician at some stage to uncover its frailties.

The process of diagnosing a business lies largely at the base of NCR selling strategy. Other elements enter into the technique of selling but practically all stem from knowledge of store weaknesses and the ability to rectify them. In short, "Find the need and meet it." When NCR production was strengthened with the imposing line of accounting machines, the same basic rule held. Banks, industries, railroads, and hotels have their accounting weaknesses. The NCR accounting machines salesman compares these weaknesses with the strength that his system provides. Selling is comparing.

It is a tribute to the man's uncanny perception of selling that many of the fundamental principles of NCR salesmanship hark back to John H. Patterson. First of all was his recognition that the selling organization is the most important single asset of the business, and that it must be trained. He pioneered, among other things, the realistic demonstration of products, the principle of "listing advantages," verbatim selling knowledge, and the constant search for new markets for the NCR output.

Patterson was the first to break down the approach to a sale into steps. He did it to expose what he called "Cash Drawer Weaknesses." He was referring to the old cash drawer under the counter. Weaknesses included no balance, no record of sales, no way to trace mistakes. In turn these weaknesses created carelessness, caused disputes and lost customers, reduced profits, and invited failure. With the baring of these basic defects began the principle of comparison of systems which remains a force in selling. Patterson devised the NCR Yard-Stick—Information, Protection, Service, Convenience, and Economy, —which is applied like a stethoscope in the analysis of store systems. This selling by comparison produces, not the traditional "deadly parallel," but a deadly contrast that leads the merchant or banker to the realization that his business needs the tonic of change. Like the intelligent patient who heeds his physician's advice when told that he has some physical defect, the wise business man takes the prescription recommended by the NCR salesman who fills the role of a doctor of business.

One of the most valuable selling legacies left by Patterson is embodied in his oft-quoted phrase: "We Teach Through The Eye," which is dramatized in many ways. One is the use of small daylight projectors by salesmen who place the machine on the desk of a prospect and flash a film on the wall. No dark room is required. The films show Why, Where, and How merchants lose money. Typical of the character of these films is the story entitled "Human Weaknesses." Another, called "Triple Play," gives a demonstration in terms of a baseball game. A third is devoted to "Food Merchandising To-day." Visual aids in the form of films and film slides are effective for both training and selling.

Here is an example of what might be called "Selling Through The Eye," told in terms of an NCR cash register salesman making a call on a druggist using a "Customer Pay-Cashier" system. The skill of observation which has become part of the salesman's approach technique through training and personal experience quickly indicates that the store can sustain financial loss through customer inconvenience, ticket manipulation, and increased operating costs. These constitute the principal weaknesses in the store system. The salesman instinctively starts to construct a store plan and system revision to eliminate the weaknesses and thereby bring about a net increase in the store profits. Dependent upon the size and type of store and other specific conditions, the salesman will either present an immediate partial analysis of the weaknesses he detects to the merchant or build his approach around a request for permission to make a complete survey of the accounting and merchandising plan in operation.

The accounting machine salesman follows the same procedure. To illustrate: When he calls on an Installment Jewelry firm he notes immediately that the hand-receipted pass-book method, with hand-written window sheet, is in use. The business, therefore, is burdened with excessive accounting costs because of the out-moded hand-posting system and inaccurate pass-book and ledger balances. He knows, too, out of his experience, observation, and training, that there must be great customer dissatisfaction due to mistakes, illegibilities, and the ever-present possibility of fraud. For these reasons he is certain that a definite need exists for an NCR Class 2000 Installment Posting System.

In order to be prepared for a proposal the salesman will ask to be allowed to make a survey of the entire system in operation. Assuming that he gets it, he will obtain first-hand information as to the number of accounts, average peak-day activity in purchases and payments, volume of business on which trade-in allowances are made, method of collection follow-up, what percentage of accounts require outside collection, and to what extent letters and other forms of "dunning" are employed. The survey will reveal every part and parcel of the business that may have a bearing on, or a relation to, a modern National system.

Surveys are not confined to individual stores or institutions, whether financial or otherwise. They cover specific lines such as the drug or grocery trades, department stores, and even entire communities. A survey of Bloomington, Ind. was made in 1942 to ascertain all the facts concerning the use of cash registers in retail stores. Every merchant in the town was interviewed on the kinds of machines used and their age, and also on the accounting systems in vogue. This data provides effective background for the selling force.

An unassailable argument for the merchant's need of information about his business is set up by an NCR survey of failures in the United States. It revealed that 81.5 per cent resulted from lack of facts about the business, or lack of control over transactions on the part of store management. This is why NCR salesmen say to merchants: "A store without information is like a clock without hands. You can tell by the swing of the pendulum that it is running but you have to guess at the time."

An NCR advertisement, addressed to grocers, printed in 1945, shows the value of surveys. Headed, "How Well Do You Know Your Business?", it reads:

"Don't mistake our meaning. We don't pretend to know more about your business than you do. But it is our job to know that part of your business that is concerned with systems.

"In your grocery store you handle money and keep records. You need facts and figures to aid you in cutting down the average cost of individual sales, keeping accurate department records, and maintaining better inventory control. All this is a matter of system. So chances are that this National fact-finding survey will save you both man hours and money.

"Alert grocers today are 'putting the question mark' upon every phase of their operation, asking themselves if their present methods are the best both for now and the future. They are making their plans now, even though it may not be possible to carry them out fully until some later date.

"The size of your store makes no difference. Without obligation to you, a National representative, experienced in the grocery field, will be glad to analyze your method of controlling the turnover of your stock, the efficiency of your clerks, and the cost of giving better service to each customer.

"After this analysis, the National representative will make recommendations in black and white as to how you can strengthen any weak points in your present system. There is no obligation."

The NCR Systems Information Department, covering both cash register and accounting machine sections, studies and develops systems, producing blueprints known as propositions. The purpose is to give the prospective customer as complete a picture as possible of just how a proposed system will operate, and what may be expected of it. Part of the work of this department is of direct selling nature and part educational for the men in the field.

Perhaps no aid to the NCR selling force is more highly organized or effective than the Merchants Service Bureau. It was set up to advise store proprietors on their problems of management, to help them meet new and changing conditions in business, and to assist in the training of their clerk personnel. Continuous research by experts provides a vast amount of useful information which is always at the disposal of merchants. In consequence, NCR has come to be regarded as one of the best informed authorities on retail operation in the United States. Its cooperation is constantly sought not only for the mass of available helpful printed material, but for talks by its market researchers to trade groups and gatherings of retail merchants. The Merchants Service Bureau operates independently of direct selling because its primary function is larger service to stores.

The book, "Better Retailing," which is copiously illustrated, is an example of the kind of educational service rendered by Merchants Service. Called a hand-book, it is really a Bible for merchants. Millions of copies have been distributed since its first publication in 1921. The eleventh edition, thoroughly revised, was brought out in 1941.

The first chapter, "Establishing a Retail Business," is typical of the completeness of the contents. It surveys the retail situation in this country, gives the reasons for retail failures, deals with personality and success, lists community opportunities, shows the amount of capital required, analyzes risk spreading, and discloses basic rules for financial success. The second chapter supplies the merchant or prospective merchant with all the necessary information about "Store Location." It includes detailed methods of finding shopping areas and estimating customer traffic and purchasing power. All the other chapters are equally informative.

Education of merchants and training of their personnel comprise only part of the function of the Merchants Service Bureau. It developed a system of approach and coverage for check-out, that is, self-service, stores unexcelled in modern salesmanship. It is no exaggeration to say that the NCR contributed largely to the set-up and equipment of this unique phase of present-day selling.

The evolution from the old-time cash drawer to the cash register is almost matched by the shift from clerk service to self-service. Under the old system a clerk was required for each customer. If the four clerks in a store were each engaged with a client, other customers were obliged to wait. The average human being is impatient of delay. Many stores lost business because they had an insufficient number of clerks.

In 1916 Clarence W. Saunders, a Memphis, Tenn. business man, originated the first of the self-service stores which launched the Piggly Wiggly chain. The idea is quite simple. Customers enter the store through a turnstile which bars egress. The customer, who selects his own purchases, is provided with a basket or a small cart in which to carry or haul them to a checker who stands at a narrow exit, and receives payment. Two checkers can handle fifty people. Within a dozen years there were over 3,000 Piggly Wiggly stores operating under franchise. The check-out store is now a nation-wide institution.

The change in shopping habits, which largely eliminated hand-to-mouth buying, accelerated the march of the check-out store. The electric refrigerator enabled the house-wife to keep meat over a considerable period while the wide use of the automobile permitted shoppers to buy in quantity and convey their purchases home easily. This meant bigger stocks and less spoilage in stores, fewer clerks, and consequently larger turn-over and bigger profit.

The trend toward check-out stores created a need on the part of merchants for an effective store lay-out. The Merchants Bureau fulfilled this requirement with a model store arrangement which invoked store engineering. The store arrangement consists of a number of miniature fixtures and a lay-out board drawn to scale. The merchant sends in a rough diagram of his proposed store giving the overall dimensions and some idea of what he has in mind. The miniature store is set up and photographed. The photograph is then sent to the merchant and becomes his guide in building the store. In six years nearly

7,000 of these lay-outs have been sent to merchants.

On the theory that "Merchandise Displayed is 75 Per Cent Sold," Merchants Service plans wide store aisles that lead customers past all the merchandise. This allows them to see and handle the goods. Easy flow of store traffic, combined with accessibility to all stock, invites more "buying on sight." Merchants Service also helps to train checkers and sackers by providing manuals for them. Its publication "Information for Merchants" covers every phase of check-out store conduct.

All this detailed aid to self-service store set-up and operation would be incomplete without an adequate accounting system. The NCR provides this with its Class 6000 itemizer machine. This is the way it operates: when the customer pays for the merchandise at the checking stand each item is recorded in the register. Thus the amount is publicly disclosed. When all the items have been recorded the machine shows the total amount purchased. This publicity enables the shopper to supervise the transaction by observing what is being charged. She knows the amount is right because it is mechanically added. The receipt, issued to the customer, prints each item bought by departments, the total, consecutive number, date, and the name and address of the merchant. When the shopper leaves the store she has a detailed record of her shopping. For the merchant there is equal protection. A printed record is retained in the register showing each item purchased, sales by departments, and the total sales for the day.

Since sales are the life blood of the business, this life-giving fluid is never allowed to become sluggish. It needs stimulants. There is no lack of them in the NCR selling organization. Once more we must go back to John H. Patterson, this time for the introduction of three vital accelerators of selling.

The first is guaranteed territory. A guaranteed territory salesman is guaranteed remuneration on any sale made in his domain. The specific benefits of this arrangement are that it places definite responsibility for selling, establishes satisfactory customer relationship, contributes to good-will building, eliminates duplication of effort and controversy over prospects and sales credit, increases money-making possibilities and stimulates long-range sales promotion.

Second is the quota which establishes a definite measure of sales efficiency and accomplishment. The District Manager allocates a quota for each man in charge of a guaranteed territory. Quota is par and is based on merchant and buying population, bank clearings, and the past record of the salesman. The salesmen are expected to make par but many exceed it.

The advantages of the quota system are manifold. For one thing it takes selling out of the realm of speculation and reduces it to a mathematical basis. In consequence, factory budget, production, and advertising can be safely scheduled. The quota also enables the company to assign and distribute responsibility for every salesman. It creates friendly rivalry which speeds up sales. Finally it establishes a basis for qualification as member of the Hundred Point Club, the NCR Legion of Honor, whose conventions are outstanding events in the lives of all the salesmen.

The Hundred Point convention was a logical outgrowth of the quota idea. It sprang from that first historic sales conference held at the Phillips House in 1886. Patterson saw how the informal sales meeting whetted sales interest so, beginning in 1887, general conventions of salesmen became an annual fixture. Nine salesmen attended the first convention. When the gavel fell in 1888, fifty-one were on hand.

Impressed by the enthusiastic reaction of the salesmen to the conventions Patterson, always the showman, decided to expand the idea. Out of it emerged the Hundred Point conventions which have provided the pattern for similar merit organizations in many companies. Membership in the Hundred Point Club —familiarly referred to as CPC—is by points. Patterson was the first industrial executive to use points. At a much later day, I might interpolate, the entire United States was on a point system, but for a different reason.

To qualify for the CPC a salesman must make his full year's quota. Each point represents $25 of sale. The minimum quota is 100 points a month or 1200 for the year. It means that the salesman is required to sell $30,000 worth of product during the twelve months to make the club. If a man's quota is 200 points a month, or 2400 points for the year, he must roll up $60,000 in business.

Seventy men answered the roll call for the first CPC convention in 1906. At the 1941 convention, the last before we entered the Second World War, the attendance was 639. Among those present were two members who had qualified 27 times; two, 26 times, and one, 24 times. The club officers are chosen from the men with the highest sales records.

Membership in the CPC induces reward and recognition in many colorful ways. The annual conventions are marked by elaborate programs. A special newspaper, replete with pictures and stories about the members and their selling achievements, is published daily during the conventions.

The CPC conventions reveal a cross-section of the most efficient elements in American salesmanship, buoyant with the NCR family spirit, and dedicated to dynamic effort. They stoke the members with enthusiasm for the selling year ahead. Sales leaders make addresses and there is always a valuable interchange of ideas. Furthermore, they inspire the men to put forth their most valiant best since consistent membership in the CPC is a first consideration in qualification for promotion. The salesmen have the same degree of pride in a high number of memberships that college men have in their Phi Beta Kappa keys.

Reinforcing all these stimulants to selling is advertising. Few companies can claim an earlier recognition of the value of advertising than the NCR. Patterson started to advertise almost as soon as he began to build cash registers. Over the years practically every type of advertising except the radio has been employed. The main effort, initiated by Patterson, has been direct mail with which a specific message can be sent to the individual merchant when it is likely to have the greatest effect. For many years a mailing list of 1,500,000 merchants was maintained at an annual cost of $50,000. This list has been reduced because the purchase of special lists has proved to be more useful. As many as 350 different pieces of advertising have been kept in stock at one time.

The NCR advertising material, especially direct mail, has always been marked by elaborate printing, high type of illustration, and imagination. Four color printing has been the rule. As early as 1900 many NCR direct mail pieces were rated as "advanced" for their day because they departed from the conventional conception of what publicity should be. Some were unique but all were effective in telling a story. One, in verse, called "The Store-Keeper's Dream," told the story of a merchant's son who, after graduating from college and entering his father's business with high hopes for the future, fell into bad company, yielded to the temptation of the open cash drawer, and finally wrecked his own life and brought disgrace upon the family. Patterson's celebrated "chalk talk" idea was used in advertising material. An early booklet, "Chalk Talks," reproduced blackboards with selling arguments written on them. One showed a man being hit by a motor car. Below him was a cash register. The text was: "You insure your life. Why not insure your money too! A National cash register will do it."

Distribution of direct mail advertising is handled in two ways. Special campaigns are planned in which material is mailed from Dayton to a selected list which may be all grocers, druggists, or hardware dealers. Distribution is also made through the sales offices in the field. Each office has an adequate supply of advertising matter but uses its own list of names. In the New York and Chicago offices 25,000 names are on the lists.

The NCR products are not mass consumer items such as automobiles, soaps, foods, and tooth paste in which practically every reader is interested. There are 1,900,000 merchants and 500,000 other types of business men in the United States who are considered prospects for NCR machines. Thus, of the 130,000,-000 people in this country, something under 3,000,000 are directly interested as probable purchasers. Because of this selectivity trade journals have been a close second to direct mail for NCR advertising since they go to specific fields of business.

From the day when Patterson showed his advertisements to a nearby German grocer to find out if he could understand them, simplicity has been the keynote of NCR advertising. Patterson felt that if this humble man could comprehend them, every one else could. It was also Patterson's praotice to call factory foremen into a meeting and get their opinion on proposed advertisements.

Patterson did not confine his advertising to the printed word. He believed in all forms of advertising. He took considerable space at world's fairs and business shows, and insisted that original and attractive window displays be maintained at all the branch offices. This policy has been followed consistently ever since. A notable NCR window display of recent years was the dramatization of Charles Dickens' "A Christmas Carol" with one-third life size figures portraying the classic story. Another display recounted the advance of accounting through the ages.

Since the NCR product involves highly specialized mechanism, the advertising must not only be specialized but geared to a great variety of applications. The company sells cash registers to 60 different kinds of retail businesses. Within these types are many variations. The grocery business, for example, which counts as only one line, includes clerk service and check-out stores, the small store and the super market, the store with a meat department and the one without. On the accounting machine side there is even a wider diversification because it serves banks, hotels, installment houses, railroads, laundries, mail order houses, insurance companies, and many other activities. When you further realize that there are more than 500 styles and sizes of NCR machines, you get some idea of the breadth of the advertising material necessary to reach all these lines.

Practically all NCR advertising is printed in the company's plant, one of the largest private printing installations in the world. The fact that it was established in 1887 is an additional indication of the early interest in printed material. The plant also prints detail strip rolls, receipt rolls, and auxiliary items used with registers. The NCR has its own photograph department, also created in 1887, which makes a pictorial record of all happenings. The result is that the company has a complete history in pictures, still and motion, of its progress almost from the first year.

Ingrained into the selling organization is the significance of the maxim, "Service and Selling are Synonymous." After superiority of product nothing is more conducive to user good will than adequate maintenance of machines. The NCR repair shops attached to the offices in the field have always maintained a high standard of service. In 1945 the service was expanded by the establishment of Service Depots at strategic points in the provincial territory. These depots do not supersede the shops maintained at the branches and sub offices. Because of their strategic location they make for quicker service and lower cost in a wider field.

Linked with the repair job is the all-important item of spare parts. During normal times this presents no difficulty. When we entered the war upkeep, so far as spare parts were concerned, bristled with complexities for all American industry. Spare parts suddenly became almost precious things.

Another problem was projected by the war. Parts can be renewed but replacement of repair men who entered the armed forces was not so easy. Out of 1914 men engaged on NCR repair, 935 went to war. Women were recruited for the work, supplementing graduates of the Repair School.

The NCR selling force in the United States is deployed through 325 branches and other offices. In this country the various Divisions are Southeastern, Northeastern, Central, Northern, Pacific and Southern, with a branch in Canada. Branch managers total 206. They are all salesmen with notable selling records to which they bring a high degree of executive ability. The NCR sales organization has established a distinguished tradition of service. It includes 333 men who have been with the company 25 years or longer.

One reason for this tradition of service is that a large percentage of successful NCR salesmen entered the service at an early age. The company has found that the men who do this, who gradually acquire a complete knowledge of the business, and who are given sufficient time to gain the necessary confidence in themselves, are the ones who have the best chance to advance. The NCR is constantly on the look-out for men of character and ambition. Some are found among college graduates. Many started with the company as office clerks in factory departments. Others have come up through the branch offices and the service end.

Field Marshal of the Selling Force is John M. Wilson, whose title is Vice-President in Charge of Sales. In him you have still another "little man with a dynamo inside." He is an outstanding example of promotion from the ranks for he has been office man, junior salesman, salesman, branch manager, division manager, and accounting machine manager. His is a conspicuous NCR "success" story.

After graduating from High School in his native East St. Louis, Ill., Wilson went to work in a semi-department store. While employed there he conceived great admiration for the National cash registers in use and the service they rendered to customers. As a result of this enthusiasm for the machines he asked the local NCR agent to give him a position as salesman. Since Wilson was then only 21 years old the manager suggested that he first serve an apprenticeship as office man, which he did.

Seated on a high stool at an old-style bookkeeper's desk, Wilson listened to sales talks and watched demonstrations made in the office by salesmen. He always felt a pang of disappointment when sales were not closed. One night he went to the store of a merchant whom a salesman had failed to sell and got his order. When he repeated this performance several times, the branch manager became convinced that his office man was wasting his time tinkering with accounts. Wilson became a full-fledged salesman, a role in which he was to play a star part.

Two years later the branch manager was transferred to Little Rock, Ark. Wilson accompanied him. The South was then in economic travail because cotton had slumped with our entry in the First World War. Every one was urged to buy a bale of cotton in order to maintain the price. Many merchants displayed bales of cotton in front of their stores. Based on his observations in the East St. Louis store Wilson realized that the money-saving value of a National cash register made its use more necessary during a period of depression than when times are prosperous. On this idea he waged such a successful selling campaign that he was promoted to the Salina, Kansas, agency where for years the company had been unable to establish a profitable business. The sales floor of his territory covered 31 counties, yet, single-handed, he made it a profitable outpost of the selling domain.

Now came the event which helped to shape the Wilson future. Because of his selling record he was asked to make a talk at a meeting of the entire sales force held in Dayton in November 1915. As usual, Patterson was present.

Wilson began his talk in this way:

"After leaving High School I started to work in a semi-department store. I soon realized that it would be a long time before I could earn enough, let alone save the money, necessary to go into business. Therefore I looked about for an opportunity to get into a business of my own. I found that I was able to go into business for myself under the most unusual circumstances in that the man who was willing to put me into business would also be working for me. This person is John H. Patterson."

With this utterance Patterson, who was seated in the front row, became all attention. His interest deepened as Wilson continued:

"If I were in the retail business for myself I would have to buy my merchandise and pay for it, whereas Mr. Patterson not only supplies me with the cash registers I sell, but he has an engineering department which is already anticipating the needs of the future for at least 15 or 20 years. If I were in business for myself and my merchandise were sold on credit, I would be obliged to borrow money with which to finance the accounts. Mr. Patterson carries all these accounts for me. If I were in business for myself I would not only be forced to plan all my own advertising but pay for it. However, Mr. Patterson has assumed this responsibility by providing me with the benefits of the finest advertising department of any company in this country. The man in business for himself must reinvest most of the profit which he earns in merchandise and new fixtures, but my profit is in cash which can be invested and pay interest to me.

"In the beginning I made the statement that Mr. Patterson is working for me. This is literally true because he is constantly thinking and working to do things which will increase the sale of our products. To that extent he is working to help me increase the sales of our products in my territory."

At this moment Patterson suddenly arose from his seat. Holding up his hand he said:

"Just a moment, young man."

Everyone of the 2500 persons in the audience including Wilson was electrified because nobody ever knew what would please or offend Patterson. The head of the company then added:

"This young man has just stated that I am working for him," and paused.

The pause intensified the already acute interest of the audience. Patterson went on:

"All of us are working for somebody. You are working for your wives and children. I feel sorry for any one who does not have some one dependent upon him. Some of you may wonder why I work as hard as I do. My personal wants, as well as the physical wants of my children, have been amply provided for. Then why do I continue to work as I do? As I have said, you have your families dependent upon you, but my family embraces all the members of the NCR family which includes not only all the thousands of employees here in Dayton but other thousands throughout the world. Mr. Wilson says I am working for him which means that I am working for each and every one of you. When he made that statement he displayed a better understanding of my objective in life than anything any one has ever said."

Not long afterward Patterson said to C. E. Steffey, then Sales Manager:

"Where is that young man who made the outstanding speech at the last sales convention? We should have him here in Dayton." Wilson was still in charge of the Salina branch.

Wilson was thereupon called into Dayton and became Special Assistant to the Sales Manager. In this capacity he travelled all over the country giving sales assistance to the men in the field. Subsequently he was named Manager of the Southern Division with headquarters in St. Louis, and later Manager of the Pacific Division, San Francisco. In 1943 he was appointed Vice President in Charge of Sales and elected to the Board of Directors.

Membership on the Board of Directors as the head of sales gives the selling organization representation with management. It is a recognition of the responsibilities of sales direction and was first made by the NCR in 1906 when F. L. Ditzler was named a director.

An interesting evolution is disclosed. There was a time when the products of the average company were turned over to the sales manager to sell. This was practically his sole function. He had virtually no part in deciding how the product was built or the way it was put out. It was not regarded as essential that he have any manufacturing knowledge.

For a variety of reasons manufacturers have come

more and more to the realization that the chief sales executive cannot adequately perform his task without a complete understanding of, and contact with, all the important component parts of the business. He must ascertain sales potentialities for the coming year, estimate the number of salesmen necessary to attain the sales objective, and anticipate expenses for sales training, and advertising. In short, he must co-ordinate the sales effort with that of the manufacturing division so that all branches work in accord. The Vice-President in Charge of Sales at the NCR, therefore, has his part in shaping policy and production.

When all is said and done, the most brilliant and effective sales strategy is unavailing if it lacks the medium of a superior product. In the last analysis "the product is the best salesman."

CHAPTER VII

Merchandising Comes of Age

NO CHAPTER in the long serial of American business is more picturesque than the one which records the evolution of retailing. It spans the era from primitive barter in remote wilderness trading posts by way of the country general store to the imposing skyscraper department store with its compact empire of trade. Part of the drama of our national economic development is bound up in this saga of merchandising. It links the peaceful commercial conquest of New England with the heroic winning of the West and its epic of the covered wagon. The trader advanced with the explorer to supply human needs and to lighten the burden of life and labor of pathfinder and pioneer.

The evolution of retailing is more than a far-flung business expansion which touches the pocketbook of every one. It is the story of big-visioned men who foresaw trade opportunities and capitalized them. From the simple cross-roads country store sprang the department store and the chain store system with ramifications that embrace the self-service establishment and the super market. Step by step, and always with innovations that changed but simplified shopping procedure, a mighty merchandising structure has been reared. In 1944 retail trade of all kinds in the United States mounted a total business of $69,-000,000,000. In cash register phraseology, this huge volume of trade was "rung up" in 1,770,335 stores representing 125 lines of business employing over 7,000,000 people.

To this cavalcade of retail progress NCR machines have made a notable contribution, meeting the needs of every phase in the evolution of merchandising. It is doubtful if the march of retailing could have been accomplished without the aid of the National cash register. To supremacy of product has been brought knowledge of store technique which has given the National Cash Register Company pre-eminence as an authority on retail operation. From the day when the first cash register was installed in a store the Company has been friend, philosopher, and guide of the retail merchant, pioneering and developing systems which are standard stabilizers and safeguards of retail business. For one thing, as I have already indicated, it aided largely in the systematization of self-service stores. It has rendered a no less conspicuous service to the simplification of department store counter transactions. In short, NCR machines are synonymous with efficiency, progress, and service wherever goods are sold.

Merchandising, as we know it today, was a long time coming of age. People are so apt to regard the highly organized retail store as a sort of natural phenomenon, like the radio, the telephone, and the motor car, that they seldom pause to realize that, like these inventions, it represents a long process of change from humble beginning.

The first retailing in America was carried on by Indians who engaged in inter-tribal trade in furs, foods, paints, pipes, arrow heads and an assortment of personal adornment such as beads and feathers. The trading post era began with the coming of the white man. He set up posts usually at the headwaters of navigable rivers. Now began the barter period. The white traders exchanged beads and other gew gaws for skins. Out of this emerged the pioneer American fur trade which laid the foundation of the Astor fortune, one of the first great accumulations of wealth in this country. The fur trade also projected the Hudson Bay Company with its romance of merchant adventurers who blazed the way for retail business through savage-infested wilds. Bitter competition between British and American fur traders was largely responsible for the War of 1812.

The early days of the nineteenth century witnessed the arrival of the character which history knows as the Yankee peddler. This humble individual played an important, if homely, part in the story of retailing. He was an itinerant store which brought merchandise to the door of the consumer. In his pack were the so-called "Yankee notions" consisting of pins, needles, razors, scissors, tin-ware, clocks, and a score of other useful commodities. The peddlers usually carried their stock in trade on their backs. Some, however, rode horses. A later development was the peddler store on wheels, a small horse-drawn cart filled with goods to dazzle and delight the rural housewife.

The tide of immigration from Europe in the first decades of the nineteenth century injected a factor into retailing which was destined to influence the larger structure of merchandising. It was the Jewish immigrant who sought sanctuary from Old World oppression in a new, free land. Thrown on his own resources in a strange country, he turned to trade and joined the ranks of the peddlers. Two in particular were the forbears of notable retail store dynasties.

The first was Lazarus Straus who emigrated from the Rhine Palatinate with his three sons, Isidor, Nathan, and Oscar. The elder Straus became a peddler in Georgia. Soon he operated a store at Talboton in that State. This obscure store marked the entry of the Straus family into American retailing. In time it extended to domination of the great New York house of R. H. Macy & Co. and its allied interests. The other peddler was Adam Gimbel, founder of Gimbel Brothers. After canvassing the Indiana countryside with a pack on his back he established a store at Vincennes, Indiana. From this expanded the chain of department stores that bear the Gimbel name in various parts of the country. It is worth noting that Collis P. Huntington, who created a railway empire, and B. T. Babbitt, later a soap king, began their business careers as Yankee peddlers.

The general merchandise store was the link between the more or less primitive retailing carried on by peddlers and trading posts, and the store that represented a degree of economic development. Unique among them was the country store which established a picturesque tradition. Famed in song, legend, and story it was a distinctive American institution.

A country store was the social as well as retail center of the community. All followed an identical pattern in that they contained a "pot-bellied" stove, a saw-dust spit box, and an open cracker barrel into which the ever-present loungers dipped at will. The store was also the exchange of village gossip and news. Affairs of state and foreign policies were debated and decided by the village wiseacres as they toasted their toes at the friendly stove and whittled wood. Every country store was a rural "emporium." Its merchandise ranged from pins and plows to patent medicines for man and beast. In an atmosphere reeking with the odors of sugar, plug tobacco, molasses, whiskey, vinegar, and onions the country merchant carried on. His shelves were rickety, he had no need to advertise, he carried all his credit accounts in his head. Despite all these crudities of operation he represented an epoch in retailing.

While the country store pursued its informal way the city retail store began to come into its own. The industrial revolution speeded up retailing. It brought increased quantity and variety of merchandise to mercantile shelves. Furthermore, the migration of workers from farm to city expanded buying power. Most of the city stores began with dry goods and gradually extended to other lines. Some of the early urban stores projected the American merchant princes, men of the stature of John Wanamaker in Philadelphia, Marshall Field in Chicago, R. H. Macy and A. T. Stewart in New York, and Eben D. Jordan in Boston. They, and their colleagues throughout the country, were largely responsible for the next important phase of retailing—the department store. It was a natural evolution. Instead of one store the department stores became scores of stores under one roof. Each department was a miniature shop "departmentized" from the rest of the establishment. The department store conception is one of the few large scale merchandising ideas that did not originate in the United States. Credit for its origin is usually given to the famous Bon Marché in Paris.

Once launched on these shores the department store made swift progress, setting the pace for advances in the technique of retailing that have helped to transform merchandising the world over. Year after year their volume of trade has expanded until, in 1944, the 4600 department stores in the United States registered a total business of $7,000,000,000, which was nearly one tenth of the entire retail turn-over in the nation.

The department store represents a mile-post in the evolution of American merchandising. It also marked the entry of the National cash register upon the larger retailing scene in a big and significant way. Prior to the expansion of the department store, the cash register had become increasingly a part of the equipment of many mercantile establishments. Frequently NCR salesmen were met with this question usually propounded by small tradesmen:

"If the National cash register is so necessary to the retailer, why don't the big stores use them?"

The time was at hand when the "big stores" would enlist the cash register for a service that was to become a factor for system and protection in department store development. To comprehend the revolution that the machine has wrought in the sales end of department store operation, it is necessary to visualize customer transactions as they were carried on prior to its advent.

Although department stores had increased mightily in size and volume of business they were handicapped by an archaic system that invited dishonesty on the part of clerks and therefore sapped profit and made for customer inconvenience and dissatisfaction. At the root of this long-standing evil lay the handwritten sales slip. It was the day of handwritten letters and bills and mentally-added figures.

The Department Store Cash System was the

method of having clerks or sales people write a memorandum of each sale showing the item purchased and the price paid for it. At the end of the day the slips were collected and added up, the total representing the amount of money which should be turned over to the proprietor. This procedure offered little assurance that the store would receive all the money.

In an effort to correct this weakness the duplicating Sales Book System was devised and used for years. It consisted of identical sales slips with a carbon between. The sale was recorded on the top slip causing a carbon duplicate to be made at the same time on the bottom slip. The clerk took the merchandise, money, and both slips to a central cashier who checked the amount on the slip with the price ticket on the goods bought. If correct she would stamp "Paid" on the sales slips, wrap the duplicate slip in the package with the purchase, hand it back with the correct change to the clerk who gave it to the waiting customer.

As department stores grew in size and the distance between counter and cashier desk increased, so-called "Cash Girls" were used as messengers. Later on mechanical messengers and pneumatic tubes were employed to convey money and merchandise to the cashier. Stores continued to expand. It meant that where there were hundreds of clerks local cashiers supplanted the central cashier.

It was at this juncture that the National cash register moved into the picture to bring efficiency and protection to the department store proprietor. Once more you have the informal beginning of a momentous advance in cash register service.

Like all other department stores the John Wanamaker establishment in Philadelphia suffered from sales slip manipulation. One summer day soon after the turn of the century Franklin N. Brewer, General Manager of the store, called a meeting of department heads to discuss the situation. To them he said:

"We must have some mechanical means to be used by our cashiers that will print in legible figures the total amount of sales slip transactions and at the same time add a total for the cashier. The device must print the cashier's number, cut off the stub, and lock it in the machine. With such a machine we can be assured a correct audit of our sales people's transactions and an accurate balance."

There was prompt response to Brewer's suggestion. One of his associates built a machine that printed the amount of the purchase on the main portion of the sales slip and also on a stub which was severed from the slip and deposited in a locked box. The main portion was to go with the goods to the customer while the stub remained in the box for the cashier. This register never reached the commercial stage. It served a useful purpose, however, because the NCR took it over and developed it into the cash register known as the Class 100.

The Class 100, or "The Black Box," as it was sometimes called, realized all that Brewer desired and much more. In a single operation the register automatically printed in unchangeable, indelible figures the amount of sale, the date, consecutive number, and the cashier number on both original and duplicate sales checks and on a stub which was cut from the duplicate slip and dropped into a locked compartment in the register. At the same time it added the amount of sale into a mechanical total. The store had a certified copy of the sale while the customer got a printed receipt of the same amount. By looking at the adding total under lock and key the proprietor knew at any time the amount of money that should be in the register drawer. Thus was overcome the weakness of the old duplicating sales slip system which had caused so much loss to the department stores. It was another link in the chain of protection that the National register forged for the merchant.

Cash transactions comprised only part of the department store business. Many stores made sales on credit. The problem was to know who was entitled to buy on credit and who was not. When stores were small it was a simple proposition to have a list of "charge customers" on file at the central cashier's desk. Charge slips could be sent there and verified. With the growth of stores and the increase in the number of cashiers it was not so simple. Again the NCR rose to the emergency, this time with the O. K. Charge Telephone, the brain child of C. F. Kettering, which was fully described in a preceding chapter. With the Class 100 Register and the O. K. Telephone, the NCR simplified and expedited cash and credit transactions.

Prior to 1910 all emphasis on cash register development, so far as department stores were concerned, was placed on added protection for the sales-slip cashier system. One evil remained. Customers were obliged to wait until packages were wrapped and change made at a cashier's desk distant from the sales counter. This procedure limited the number of patrons a clerk could serve and resulted in delay and dissatisfaction. The buying public dubbed the system "department store red tape" and chafed at it. Furthermore, the expense of maintaining cashier-wrappers and inspectors added greatly to store overhead.

After careful study and considerable pioneering the NCR devised the Clerk-Wrap register—the Class 500—which revolutionized cash handling methods in department stores and opened up a new field for the sale of the highest grade of cash registers. This machine was equipped with a detail strip which superseded the chopped-off stub indicators, a slip printer, receipt printer, multiple drawers, and multiple totals. It gave publicity to sales, provided a history of each transaction, and reenforced protection.

The clerk took the customer's money, rang up the sale on a register in which she had her own drawer, wrapped the parcel, handed the change and a receipt to the patron. Each clerk, therefore, became her own cashier. Such was the operation of the Standard-Clerk-Wrap machine the basis of all present-day department store cash registers.

Subsequent developments produced the Class 2000 Register with 27 individual totals and 3 grand totals, which enabled a clerk to sell in more than one department and issue a single receipt showing item by item as well as the total. This was the first streamlined machine with all mechanism enclosed. Another development is expressed in the Class 6000 register with its improved control which puts a further check on possible manipulation.

The National cash register has also played a large part in the systematization of another miracle of American merchandi ing—the chain store. Called "the team mate of ma s production," the chain store has become a distinct feature of our shopping life. No phase of retailing, save perhaps the "Five and Ten," so represents the democratic idea in retailing. The chain store caters alike to rich and poor, bringing an astonishing variety of commodities within the reach and purse of all the people.

The average housewife who makes a daily or bi-weekly visit to her favorite chain store scarcely realizes the extent of the business to which she contributes. The store she patronizes is one of 123,195 chain establishments. They are units in 6500 different chains—a chain is four or more stores—stretching from coast to coast that accounted for a total business of $15,000,000,000 in 1944.

The chain store seems to be so essentially a part of ultra-modern business organization that it is difficult to realize that the idea harks back to the Middle Ages. The Fuggers, who founded Germany's first great mercantile and banking hierarchy in the fifteenth century, set up branches for the distribution of their products throughout the globe. The letters to the parent office from correspondents provided one of the earliest sources of world news. In the seventeenth century the Mitsuis then, as today, Japan's mightiest business and financial dynasty, operated a chain of apothecary shops. The oldest chain service on the American continent was established by the Hudson Bay Company in 1670. Their fur trading centers were the outposts of a great commercial enterprise which is still going strong. It stems from frontier log-cabin "factories," as they were called, in the Canadian wilderness to modern department stores that express the last word in present day merchandising.

The chronicle of the origin and expansion of chain stores in the United States is packed with the romance of self-made success. It is the story of men of large vision and abiding faith in an idea who expanded small undertakings into nation-wide empires of retail distribution.

The pioneer chain store system in the United States was launched in circumstances typical of the birth of many kindred organizations. The scene was a small hide and leather store down on Vesey street in New York City conducted by George F. Gilman. The year was 1859, a time pregnant with meaning for the nation. Already the storm clouds of the Civil War brooded over the horizon. It was also a year fraught with significance for American retailing.

One of Gilman's employees was George H. Hartford, a taciturn, bearded Yankee. Although short on speech, he was articulate with ideas. One of them gave him a niche in our economic history.

Like so many of his countrymen Hartford was a consumer of tea. Having an inquiring mind, to say nothing of a thrifty Yankee instinct, he began to look into the cost and mechanics of tea selling. At that time tea sold around $1 a pound. Hartford believed that this worked a serious hardship on the poorer classes. All the tea retailed in this country was sold through middle men, whose part in the operation kept the price up.

Hartford, with Gilman as associate, decided to cut costs by buying tea direct from China. With the Great American Tea Company he put his plan into effect. He not only brought the price of tea down to 30 cents a pound but established the first link in what, in time, became a famous food chain. Thus tea again made a contribution to American history. The Boston Tea Party, historic protest against "taxation without representation," was a prelude to the Revolutionary War. Hartford's tea store initiated a cycle of merchandising.

When Gilman withdrew from the business Hartford assumed sole command. It was Hartford's showmanship that caused the first tea chain store to be painted a bright red flecked with gold. It became a sort of trade-mark for the chain. Once in control Hartford made expansion the watchword. By 1900, when 200 stores were linked and when groceries had been added to the first stock item of tea, the original corporation title was replaced by the more expansive appellation of The Great Atlantic and Pacific Tea Company—the familiar "A & P" of contemporary retailing nomenclature.

Today, with sons of the founder dominating the business, the "A & P" conducts 6,000 stores which sell 8 per cent of all the food sold at retail in the United States. The one-time small economy store has been extended to larger establishments which account for one-tenth of the chain store business.

Nineteen years after Hartford opened his first "Red Front" tea store in New York, an eight dollar a week clerk in the Moore & Smith Store in Watertown, New York, conceived the idea of piling a miscellaneous lot of slow selling merchandise on a table bearing the sign, "Any Article Five Cents." Shoppers literally grabbed at the opportunity. The table was cleared in short order. The enterprising young clerk was Frank W. Woolworth. The success of his bargain table, and particularly the one price of the goods, gave him the inspiration for what became the pioneer variety store chain that added the name of Woolworth to the shopping vocabulary.

Following the success of his bargain table sale Woolworth decided to develop the idea on his own. With a small loan from his Watertown employer he opened a "Five Cent Store"—the first in the United States—at Utica, New York. The people of Utica did not respond to the Woolworth fixed price invasion. Before long the youthful merchant closed up shop. Undeterred, he disposed of his stock and started another Five Cent Store at Lancaster, Pa. Fortune now favored him. He sold nearly half of his merchandise in two days. Within a year he opened a second store at Harrisburg, Pa. where his younger brother, C. S. Woolworth, joined him. In 1883 the Woolworths increased the maximum price of their merchandise to ten cents inaugurating the now familiar "Five and Ten" stores. These two stores were the forerunners of the 2,000 retail units that bear the Woolworth name throughout the country.

The word "variety" is no misnomer when applied to a Woolworth store. There are 4613 different items in the average stock of each establishment. The Woolworth stores have become international in scope. There are chains in Great Britain, Canada, Germany, and Cuba. Like the National cash register, the Woolworth store has become a world citizen.

The chain store tradition has been worthily carried on by the men who followed in the wake of Hartford and Woolworth, men of the type of J. G. McCrory, S. S. Kresge, S. H. Kress, Frank Melville,

Jr., B. H. Kroger, J. C. Penney, W. T. Grant, George J. Whelan, Charles R. Walgreen, G. C. Murphy, J. J. Newberry, Marion Skaggs, H. L. Green, and Louis K. Liggett.

One of the comparatively recent additions to the American chain store systems are the units established by the great mail order houses of Montgomery Ward & Co. and Sears Roebuck & Co. Many large department stores are also linked in chains. Whether national, sectional, or local the chain store has added materially to the expansion of merchandising and given mass sales a definite impetus.

That latest marvel of merchandising—the super market—deserves a section all its own. Designated by one of its historians as "a combination of the old trading post, the country general store, and a chain store," it embodies features of unique interest. Although its mushroom growth covers a little more than a decade, it is not a recent retail phenomenon. Up to 1932 practically all super markets were confined to the Pacific Coast. They began as "drive in" markets which were open air shopping centers for the automobile trade. The West Coast climate and the motor-shopping habits of the people made this type of merchandising easy and accessible. The stores were large arenas where people wandered at will to choose their purchases from multitudinous stocks. The self-service system prevailed.

The super market was somewhat tardy in its invasion of the eastern section of the country. It was

not until 1932 that two super markets blazed the trail
on the Atlantic Seaboard. Climate and shopping
habits were not contributory causes as was the case
in the West. Millions of men and women were un-
employed; family budgets had shrunk. Stark economic necessity, born of the depression travail, made
it imperative for the average housewife to stretch the
food dollar to the limit. Another factor entered.
Vast piles of so-called "distress merchandise," that
is, goods that could find no purchasers, were piled
up in warehouses.

Two energetic men, both born showmen with long
chain store experience, capitalized the troubled situation. One was Michael Kullen; the other was Roy
O. Dawson. They employed identical spectacular
methods in getting their retailing ideas over to the
public.

Kullen started the King Kullen Market—"The
World's Greatest Price Wrecker," as he called it—
at Bellaire, Long Island, in a huge abandoned ga-
rage. The vast size of the place lent itself to the
super market conception in that Kullen could display an immense stock of distress merchandise. The
old familiar slogan, "Price No Object," ruled. Goods
were almost given away. Kullen's circus advertising
attracted thousands from near and far. Before long
Kullen had a chain of super markets on Long Island.

Dawson was no less sensational in his methods. In
association with Robert Otis he rented the vacant
Durant automobile factory at Elizabeth, New Jersey,

stocked it with a prodigious amount of distress commodities, and opened the doors to a public eager to snap up bargains, not only in food but paints, radios, hardware, drugs, soft drinks, meats, and automobile accessories. Dawson named his first store "The Big Bear Super Market—The Price Crusher."

Crude was the word for those early super markets whether in the East or West. The fixtures were cheap, giving the stores a bazaar-like appearance. Stocks were often piled high on pine tables. The super market customers cared nothing for store style. What they wanted was low-priced and accessible merchandise and they got it.

Out of the mining camp era, for such it was, the super market has evolved into a standardized segment of American retail merchandising. The distinctive features are the large size of the stores, departmentization, lavish display of stock, and conspicuous advertising. Some super markets are independent; others are linked in chains. All incorporate the feature of combined warehousing and retailing. Many of the original chains now include super market units. Mass merchandising and mass sales are the key-notes of super market progress, as the total business in 1944 attests. The 7980 super markets sold $2,000,000,000 worth of goods.

Despite the advance of the department store, the chain store, and the super market the independent store retains its numerical advantage. Of the grand total of 1,770,335 retail stores throughout the country, the independents represent 1,624,665. They include the neighborhood store, that friendly haven of the shopper with its personal service, whether in metropolitan area or smaller community.

What of the future of merchandising? Already the idea of mechanized merchandising is passing from dream stage to some degree of reality. Retailing has travelled far since the country store first began to purvey the public. It is likely to travel much farther under the stimulus of fresh demand. Whatever the future trend, National machines will be in the van of the procession of progress.

CHAPTER VIII

The Revolution in Accounting

THERE was a time when the office was the step-child of business. Since it did not produce a profit it was generally regarded as a necessary evil, something to be tolerated. Every other activity of a firm had priority over the bookkeeping department which was usually stuck away in a dank and dingy corner. The bookkeeper of the old school was the original forgotten man. Perched on a stool at a high desk, with a green shade over his eyes, he was familiar, if unsung, figure of other days. Laboriously he kept his accounts in a day book, a journal, and a general ledger, copying letters in a canvas-bound book of tissue sheets, the old-time letter press. He embodied the mechanics, such as they were, of the era of handwritten records. In primitiveness these records matched the period of the cash drawer under the counter. One made for inaccuracy and manipulation of accounts; the other was an invitation to theft. Both impeded business profit and progress.

Just as the National cash register brought system and protection to retail business, so did modern equipment open the way to the transformation of the business office and the eventual mechanization of bookkeeping. The typewriter and the adding machine pioneered the approach. In turn came carbon paper which put the letter press into the discard; the loose leaf system with mechanical binder and loose leaf ledger which supplanted bound book records; the card index which made for quick reference; and the locked steel filing cabinet with its stability and security. Each of these innovations, looked upon with disfavor at the start, represented a step toward office stabilization. Another step remained.

During all this evolution in equipment the merchant and the manufacturer looked for three things. The first was reduction of man labor; second was the lowering of operating costs to be reflected in a reduced price of product and an increased market; third was accurate, systematized information which would enable management to formulate policies and make adequate decisions. The mechanization of accounting achieved these three objectives. It has made the office a source of profit and it produced the all-essential information. The one-time tolerated office, figuratively, became a Cinderella, transformed into a Business Princess, shedding light and providing utility and service. The NCR waved the magic wand, so to speak, that helped to bring about this transformation. It symbolized the revolution in accounting.

Up to 1921 the NCR had concentrated on cash registers, progressively improving every type of machine and widening their scope of service. The multi-total principle subtracted as well as added and provided three classifications. There were totals for individual sales people, kinds of transactions, and departments. It represented an advanced idea for it meant adding two or three totals simultaneously.

Now was evolved the Class 2000 machine which had three sets of totals, or thirty in all. The register printed on inserted forms, thus widening its scope of work. It had a flexibility that permitted the handling of intricate retail business applications. The register was further equipped with new style indicators which could be more easily read from both the front and rear.

The Class 2000 has been explained in detail not only because it represented the highest type of cash register yet made but because it marked an epoch in NCR history. Soon it became obvious that this register could be employed for uses other than retail business. With a little engineering it became, as I previously termed it, a Mother of Machines. From it sprang the line of NCR accounting machines which are today the trusted friends and servants of business, banking, and industry.

The first offspring of the Mother of Machines was the analysis machine which launched the NCR into the accounting machine field. It has manifold uses. Basically it enables a business to make a com-

plete and direct distribution of every type of record,
vouchers, invoices, or other kindred items without
the necessity of sorting. At the end of the run of
items the machine furnishes thirty first hand totals
by departments and items and also separates the
counts of individual items. The machine virtually
puts thirty adding machines under the control of
one keyboard and operator.

The analysis machine was first used by a famous
film company to record the business of a number of
small producing companies whose output it handled.
The second user was a big mail order house. The
firm, like all others of its kind, received a daily flood
of payments in cash, checks, money orders, and
stamps. In the accurate recording and tabulating
of these payments the analysis machine performed
another useful function, that of remittance control.

Packing houses are large users of the analysis
machine. It is particularly valuable for route analysis. The machine shows just what each salesman
sells by items, that is, ham or bacon, by cost and sales
price. It renders the same service for wholesale
grocers in that it analyzes sales by salesmen and product. With the analysis machine the ice cream manufacturer can keep tab on the number and quantity of
flavors sold; the laundry proprietor is able to control
all batches of pick-up washing as well as collections
on bills paid on the route. The machine is also invaluable in State and Municipal Tax Offices for
cash certifying.

A Hungarian restaurant waiter rings up his sale

Fresh foods, fruits and vegetables are carried by this traveling fruit vendor in Holland who finds his National Cash Register invaluable

A National Cash Register in use in a shop in China

The NCR product in the National Bank of Greece in Athens

A National Cash Register rings up sales in a French butcher shop

The Pope on his way to dedicate the Commissary in Vatican City which is equipped with a National Cash Register

Old and new methods of transporting National Cash Registers
are used to haul National machines in Venezuela

A typical Class 3000 installation in a British factory office

The National Cash Register in use in faraway Singapore

A Class 6000 slip printer takes care of all the receipts in this London milk bar

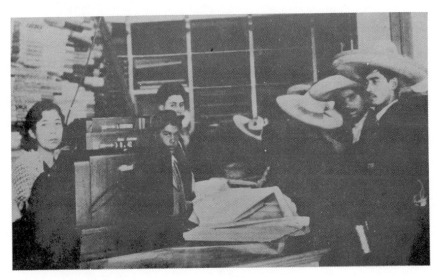

The proprietor of this dry goods store in Mexico has proper control of his cash receipts with a National Cash Register

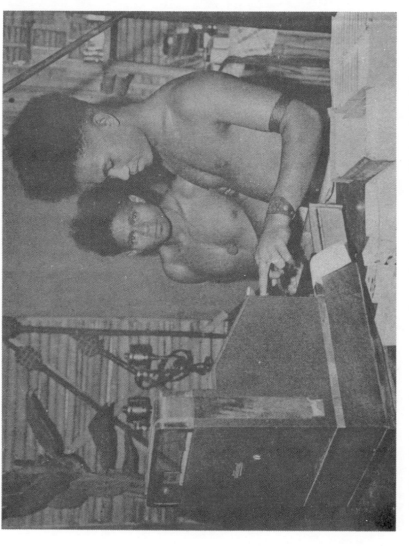

In New Guinea a fuzzy-wuzzy native makes change on a National Cash Register used in a post exchange

The analysis machine was the forerunner of a succession of NCR accounting machines that simplify, expedite, and systematize practically every phase of accounting. Through them bookkeeping has ceased to be an onerous chore emerging through mechanization as a highly efficient feature of business. The NCR accounting machine is the Nemesis of pen and pencil records.

One of the earliest of NCR accounting systematizers was the Hotel Posting machine. With it you have an illuminating "before and after using" demonstration. Nearly every one has been a guest at an American hotel at one time or another. It is no great tax on memory to recall the difficulty often experienced in getting a bill especially when you were in a hurry to catch a train. Delay, and not infrequently inaccuracy, marked the procedure.

The fundamental cause, of course, was the handwritten record which lent itself to error and manipulation. Records of charges whether for valet, porter, service, restaurant, or laundry were kept by a night clerk. The copying of handwritten guest charges on so-called night transcript sheets required time and effort for the preparation of departmental earnings and outstanding guest balances. The time consumed in making out an itemized and totaled bill for a guest when he checked out caused congestion at the cashier's window. These weaknesses meant lack of control in hotel accounting. They created ill will, and increased overhead expenses.

The NCR Hotel Posting machine changed all this. It swept away the antiquated and cumbersome handwritten record with all its inaccuracy and inconvenience. It posts guests' account cards and bills—there is an itemized daily ledger card for each guest —at the cashier's window in the front office. As a by-product of this posting a definite control is established over all charges and credits. The machine prints verification of posting on the posting voucher and also prints a detailed record of each posting on the audit sheet—all in one operation. Under this system there is no need for the cashier to write up all checkouts and disbursements to secure a cash balance because these individual totals are accumulated within the machine.

In this way both hotel management and patron are benefited. The hotel has a complete, dependable and up-to-the-minute record of the guest's business; the guest gets an itemized bill almost the moment he asks for it.

The Hotel Posting machine did more than bring speed, control and system into hotel accounting. It led to another important advance in NCR accounting machines. The NCR engineers found that with slight changes in the mechanism it could be made to print the record of a deposit in a depositor's pass book and on the bank's ledger card by the same operation. With the Bank Posting machine—the first of its kind—began a new day in savings bank accounting and service to the depositor.

To understand the great change brought about by the Bank Posting machine we must again go back to the weaknesses of the handwritten record. Nowhere was the system more destructive of time and accuracy perhaps than in savings banks. It was so slow that often depositors were forced to wait in queues. This consumed valuable time both for bank employees and clients.

The defects of the handwritten system in savings banks were many. An error made in a pass book when entering the amount deposited remained unknown to the bank for some time. When discovered it became a cause of dispute. A teller could hold out a deposit slip and the accompanying cash without the knowledge of the bank because the deposit slip was the bank's only record of the transaction after the depositor left the window. There was nothing to enforce the making of a handwritten record. The record could be miscalculated, changed, withheld, destroyed, or lost. Finally, handwritten records could not be depended upon to give management complete control.

The Bank Posting machine eliminates these weaknesses. It records the transactions on both pass book and ledger card with a single operation. Pass book and ledger, therefore, always agree. At the time the posting is made a complete journal-audit strip is printed in the exact order that each deposit takes place. The records are automatically distributed and classified by individual totals, retained under lock and key to be cleared only by an authorized auditor. Even when cleared all the information is in printed form and cannot be changed without detection. Protection bulwarks speed and accuracy.

Window posting by the NCR machine means that all the bookkeeping is done at the window while the patron is there. It provides him or her with a neat and businesslike record of the deposit and gives the bank a continuous, running, and infallible audit. Furthermore, it prevents lobby congestion, provides better customer service, and eliminates back office posting. Not only are fewer clerks required but after-office-hour work is precluded. The result is satisfied personnel. The operation of the Bank Posting machine costs approximately three cents a year per account. Hence to efficiency is added economy.

In view of the virtues that have been listed it is not surprising that the NCR Bank Posting machine is in universal use, not only through the United States but in many countries overseas. Eighty-five per cent of all savings accounts in New York State are recorded on them.

The Bank Posting machine duplicates its savings bank service for installment firms, hotels, building and loan associations, hospitals, credit unions, finance corporations, mail order houses, and many other lines of business. Wherever installed it means the end of the drudgery of handwritten records, waste effort, and inaccurate information. Another NCR accounting machine posts commercial bank deposit ledgers and makes out the monthly statements of depositors.

Since I have dealt with the Bank Posting machine it may be well to round out the cycle of NCR bank machines. This brings us to one of the miracles of mechanized accounting, the Bank Proof machine. It is a valuable contribution to banking and is the remedy for banking's greatest bugaboo, the bottle-neck in the proof department. To "prove" a bank's transactions all the transactions of a given day must be balanced.

Before the introduction of the Bank Proof machine a shortage of one cent would keep clerks up all night trying to locate the deficit. This was only one con-tribution to the troubles of clerks. Deposit slips were often incorrect. Frequently a depositor listed an item in a deposit and failed to include it in his total or vice versa.

The automatic error detector feature of the Bank Proof machine is almost uncanny in its operation. If items distributed to their various classifications agree with the total on the deposit slip the mechanism pro-ceeds smoothly to perform its task. If there is the slightest error the machine automatically stops and becomes inoperative. The error must be adjusted before the next credit can be entered. The Proof machine, therefore, becomes an inanimate watchman on the constant and unfailing lookout for mistakes. It not only finds, but corrects them.

As NCR accounting machines expanded in scope it became evident that one important service was lacking. Department stores and other lines of business needed what is termed "description" on machines, a record of items bought whether fur coats, shirts, shoes, dresses, lingerie or gloves. Description was only possible with the aid of a typewriter. The need was realized with a machine that met this requirement.

Only one machine, outside the NCR organization, had the basic typewriter-bookkeeping feature that would bring full description into the fold of service. It was manufactured by the Ellis Adding Typewriter Company. The owners, aware of their limitations in engineering and distribution, were interested in having their product adopted by the NCR. The purchase of the Ellis Company was effected in 1928. With the acquisition of the Ellis machine by the NCR another era in mechanized accounting opened.

Following this transaction came the first blending of machine strains under the aegis of the NCR. Heretofore, every machine put out by the company was undiluted NCR blood, as it were. Now an outside strain was injected. The result of the merging was what came to be known as Class 3000, the first NCR hybrid. It is a bookkeeping machine with typewriting and adding machine features. Well named "the all purpose machine," its great flexibility enables it to perform any known accounting operation. It is practical for a large field ranging from breweries and wholesale millinery establishments to department stores and steamship lines. It embodies possibilities of unlimited description. As some one said of this feature: "It narrates."

The Class 3000 is equipped with a standard typewriter and an 81 key adding machine keyboard. The advantage of this equipment is that any person who can use a typewriter or can operate an adding machine is 75 per cent trained to man it.

One feature will indicate the great flexibility of the Class 3000. By changing a form bar the function can be altered from "accounts receivable" to "accounts payable." Included in its variety of applications are payroll, daily statement, stock records, cost accounting, and general ledger.

Among other things the NCR accounting machines have greatly simplified public utility billing for gas, telephone, water or sewage service. Every Bell Telephone Company bill sent out in the United States is made on an NCR machine. Telephone users have long been familiar with the Bell monthly statement with its stub to be returned with the check. This reference to checks brings to notice the NCR check-writing machine, another aid to business. Millions of dividend checks are issued on this time and labor saving mechanism.

The problem of the payroll has existed for thousands of years. In ancient times grain, salt, wine, and live stock provided the equivalent of the contemporary pay check. Methods of paying workers have undergone a vast change but the payroll must

still be met. The system of handling it is a vital
accounting consideration for any business.

Within the last two decades the demands on payroll preparation have increased enormously. First
came the income tax. This was a trifle, so far as
labor is concerned, when compared with the deluge
of items that now clutter payrolls. Social security
led the way for the second stage of deductions which
include withholding tax, Red Cross, War Bonds,
community chest, group insurance, relief association,
and sometimes credit union, all combining to make
employers more payroll conscious. It enforced the
keeping of records more voluminous than ever
before. Information, so essential to business conduct,
took on a new value and meaning.

Always alert to changing business needs, the NCR
produced its Payroll machine, another marvel of
mechanized accounting which has taken the head-
ache out of payroll preparation. Its features include
separate totals for different types of deductions and
the ability to show on each employee's check the
gross pay, the amount and type of each deduction,
the net pay, and at the same time keep all this classified within the machine. It represents a revolutionary development in payroll accounting by reducing
the time and labor involved and furnishing accuracy
and completeness of records not previously possible.

Although it contains 17,000 parts the Payroll
machine is operated with the greatest ease, and
stands up under the most terrific pressure of work.

It is not uncommon, on an industrial payroll, to have the machine continuously computing and operating on three shifts, or twenty-four hours a day. It serves a payroll of 200,000 as readily as one of 500 workers.

When people watch the operation of the Bank proof or the Payroll machine they are apt to exclaim in wonder: "Why these machines do everything but talk!" As a matter of fact they *do* talk because they tell those responsible, whether in industry, banking or merchandising, what is important for him to know about his business. In this knowledge lies power, profit, and progress.

For years NCR salesmen were repeatedly asked: "Do you sell adding machines?" It was obvious that the adding machine fitted into the NCR pattern of product and service. Although the Class 3000 embodies the adding machine feature there was need of a low-priced adding machine to be operated on its own. While many kinds of adding machines were on the market one in particular offered the advantages that the Company demanded. This was the Allen-Wales machine. In 1943 the Allen-Wales concern was acquired by NCR becoming a wholly-owned subsidiary. The Allen-Wales machine rounded out the NCR line of accounting machines which today provide mechanization for all accounting.

Recognition of the service rendered by account-

ing machines came after the United States was
plunged into the Second World War. With the outbreak of hostilities conservation of raw materials
became imperative. Early in 1942 a ban was placed
on the production of cash registers. No accounting
machines could be made save for the Army, Navy
and the Maritime Commission.

By the end of 1942 such pressure was brought to
bear by industry, banking, government departments,
hotels, and wholesalers for the resumption of accounting machine manufacture that the War Production
Board made a survey of the situation. It showed
that the accounting machine saved 10 times the
amount of labor required to build it. If a machine
took 300 hours to build it saved 3000 man hours of
work. The survey further revealed that there had
been an increase of 20 per cent in accounts and an
expansion of 60 per cent in business all due to war
pressure. Hotels were jammed, stores crowded,
industry boomed. The famine of trained employees
due to the demands of the armed forces emphasized
the acute need for accounting machines to expedite
and simplify the work of men and women.

Late in 1942 manufacturers of accounting
machines were permitted to engage in production
for essential business. The allocation represented
about one half of normal sale. Priorities for con-
sumers were fixed by the War Production Board.
The accounting machine resumed its indispensable

place in industry and business. During the following year the demand for machines was so great that the quota for production was again increased until it was almost normal. Conservation of man power was proved to be more important than conservation of raw materials.

CHAPTER IX

A World Citizen

WITHIN a year after he established himself in the cash register business John H. Patterson was selling his product abroad. It was a procedure eminently characteristic of the man and his methods. The machine that he was destined to project into universal use was in its infancy, encountering bitter sales resistance at home. Yet, from the start, Patterson's vision beheld its wide application with the whole world as its ultimate field. He lived to see the NCR overseas organization develop into a community of nations linked by common business systems and safeguards. National machines function in fifty foreign currencies but all speak the same language of service and protection.

The first outpost of the far-flung NCR empire of business was England. In 1885 J. W. Allinson became sales representative at Liverpool. He had seen a self-adding-wheel cash register in Chicago while on a business trip to the United States. After learning that it could be adapted to English currency he ordered one. It gave such satisfaction that he decided to have a hand in selling registers. His appointment as agent at Liverpool followed. Soon afterwards William Parnall was named agent at Bristol. In 1886 Allinson's territory was extended to include all the British Isles, France, Belgium, and Holland. The first NCR presentation in England was in 1886 when cash registers were used at all the refreshment stands at the International Exposition held at Liverpool. Two years later there was a display of National registers at the Melbourne Exposition where they attracted much attention. Before the end of the eighties general agents for the NCR had been appointed in Argentina, Uruguay, Brazil, Germany, Austria, Sweden, Italy, Spain, France, and Norway.

Patterson was never a believer in absentee direction. He delighted to be on the spot when things were expanding. During the early nineties began what became his almost constant commuting to Europe. He galvanized agents with his dynamic energy, reorganized offices, made sales talks, and held his dearly beloved conventions. Not until his second trip in 1895 did he set in motion the larger plan which became the pattern of the entire NCR overseas set-up. The general agency in England was cancelled and the National Cash Register, Limited, of England was incorporated with a capital stock of £5,000. with a manager in London. Subsequently the capital was increased to £100,000.

During the formative years of the organization of the foreign field Patterson was here, there, everywhere. In 1897 he established something of a travel record. Within the space of sixty days he visited fifty cities in fifteen different countries. Wherever he went he left the impress of indefatigable effort and high speed organization. From 1908 until 1910 he was in personal charge of the London branch. Here he set up replicas of the model stores that he had used so successfully in sales training in Dayton. In 1910 H. C. Banwell became London manager.

The British NCR scene, particularly during the first part of the new century, is rich in Patterson anecdote. A convention of salesmen had been in progress in London for some days when he rose abruptly and said, "We are doing a lot for the sales force but nothing for the inside staff. We must give a luncheon for them." The Advertising Manager had exactly three hours in which to arrange a luncheon for 150 persons, but he managed to do it. Soon after the staff left for the luncheon a violent rain storm broke. Patterson then said, "Those people will get soaking wet. Each one must have an umbrella." Once more the Advertising Manager went into action, securing 150 umbrellas which he delivered to the staff at the luncheon room. Before the day was over Patterson included the families of the staff in his beneficence by ordering 150 boxes of chocolates for them. He insisted that the sweets be packed in durable boxes which could be used for gloves and handkerchiefs.

One day Patterson saw some fine old silver candlesticks in a window in Duke Street. He liked them so much that he purchased them for £20, paying cash down and ordering them sent to the office. They arrived in due course with a bill for £20. Patterson went immediately to the shop where he declared that he had paid for the candlesticks. When the shop-keeper apologized profusely Patterson said, "No, no. It is my fault. I, the President of The National Cash Register Company which makes a selling point of the value of receipts for customers, should have demanded a receipt." He insisted upon paying again but this time he got a receipt.

In the summer of 1912 Patterson did a character-istic job of neighborhood house cleaning in Totten-ham Court Road where the Company offices were located. While walking down the Road Patterson was depressed by the slovenly appearance of the district. Forty shops were vacant. When he reached the office he said to Banwell, "Empty shops are a bad advertisement for the Company. We should improve the appearance of Tottenham Court Road or move to a more prosperous area."

Patterson had held window display contests in Dayton and elsewhere in the United States so he decided to duplicate them in London. He called a meeting of neighborhood tradesmen, told them that the Company was willing to pay the cost and assist in the organization of a window display contest, and offer prizes to successful contestants. The proposal was enthusiastically received. Patterson then stated that he would also give prizes for the best dressed empty shops. This time he had hearty response from the landlords of the premises. They cleaned the shops, washed down the fronts, and in some instances painted or varnished the fronts. When the contest opened in December Tottenham Court Road was gay with flags, garlands, and bunting. Large crowds gathered to see the displays; the newspapers printed notices about them. One result was that by mid 1913 all but seven of the forty one-time vacant shops had been rented. Tottenham Court Road got a new lease on prosperity.

The window display contest in Tottenham Court Road was followed by similar contests in other sections of London, and in the provinces. From the first one developed the idea of "Shopping Week" which proved to be profitable for 300 retail areas throughout the British Isles. In Cardiff 13,000 shops participated in a "Shopping Week" which increased store sales by £40,000. The NCR office in London gave assistance to many of the communities that organized "Shopping Weeks."

Patterson delivered his factory welfare talk, in many British cities. Once, when giving it in London, a burly Englishman got up and said to him: "It is well and good for a rich corporation like yours to engage in welfare but how can I do such things? I have a lunch room with four employees." Patterson asked him for his name and address and went on with his lecture. The following day he had lunch in the man's lunch room. The proprietor was out so Patterson was able to cross-examine the waitress who served him. From her he learned that the pay was almost incredibly low, that the girls had to go outside for their meals and pay for them, that the work hours were long, and that the employees were compelled to walk great distances to their homes in order to save a few pennies.

Patterson went to the Continent. On his return to London he delivered the welfare lecture before a large meeting. In the course of the talk he told of the conditions that he had found in the lunch room. The proprietor was present. When Patterson gave the lecture again and once more told about the lunch room, the owner rose and said, "I am the man that the speaker has described." He then stated that, as a result of Patterson's talk, he had raised the pay and shortened the hours of his employees and allowed them to have their meals in the lunch room at cost.

Having entrenched the NCR firmly in England Patterson turned to the Continent with Germany as the first objective. Here he established the second link in what became an overseas corporate chain. In October 1895 The National Cash Register Company m.b.H. was organized with G. H. Wark, then head of the Brooklyn office, as manager. Subsequently Wark became European manager.

Patterson took full command of the European situation extending Company operations until they embraced every major continental country. The old general agency plan was abandoned completely in Europe. Instead, subsidiary companies were established in France, Austria, Belgium, and Spain. Within a decade the name of NCR was emblazoned on show room fronts and office windows from London to Rome. Meanwhile the foreign organization had extended to Mexico, Argentina, and the West Indies where general agents were appointed. In 1896 Patterson was able to hold his first international convention in Dayton. The first convention of German agents was held in Berlin the following year. By the time the nineteenth century had gotten under way National cash registers were recording sales in rupees-annas; marks-pfennings; rubles-kopeks; francs-centimes; lira-centissimi; gulden-cents; yen-sen; in fact nearly every known currency.

As the overseas organization expanded to world-wide proportions two important shifts were made in the plan of operation. The first, ordered by Patterson, was to change the name of the various subsidiary companies from The National Cash Register Company, that is, the title in English, into the language of the country where the company functioned. Thus the German corporation became *National Registrier Kassen Ges. m.b.H.;* the French company emerged as *La Nationale Caisse Enregistreuse S.A.;* the Spanish, *Cajas Registradoras 'National';* and the Italian, *Societa Anonima Registratori di Cassa 'National.'*

The usual Patterson practicality was evident in

this change. So long as the name of the company was in English the cash register was invested with something of a foreign atmosphere. Despite the great service it rendered, it was an alien. With the name of the company in the language of the country, some of the "outside" flavor was removed. Patterson was an internationalist and always impressed upon his overseas representatives the need of conforming their methods and operations to local customs and conditions.

The second change was in line with sound selling policy. In the early years Americans were sent to manage the foreign companies. Although highly capable some of them did not always comprehend the psychology of the people with whom they dealt. This was particularly true in the Latin countries of Europe and in Latin America. Latins superseded the Americans in many instances. Today an Argentine is in charge in Chile and Brazil; a Chilean in Mexico; a Cuban in Colombia; a Cuban heads the Caribbean area.

Although the overseas organization conforms to local customs and conditions, American methods of organization and selling are in force everywhere. Sales schools were established in London, Zurich, Milan, Brussels, Stockholm, Batavia, Sydney, Melbourne, Wellington, N.Z., Johannesburg, Buenos Aires, Sao Paulo, Rio de Janiero, Havana, Bogota, and Mexico City. Before the Second World War schools flourished in Berlin and Tokio. One of the postwar plans is for a school for all Europe in Zurich or Paris in charge of Dayton-trained men. There will also be one at Havana for Latin American salesmen. The course in all the overseas sales schools is eighteen months, longer than in the United States, because the foreign salesmen go directly into the school and not after some experience in the field as obtains over here. The overseas organizations conduct repair schools patterned after the parent repair school in Dayton. It has its own publication, "Overseas Systems and Selling Helps."

A merit system in overseas selling duplicates the American point plan. Europe, Latin America, the Far East, and The Antipodes have their Hundred Point Clubs and conventions. A point overseas is equivalent to $25 in the currency of the country where the sale is made. An Englishman, Frenchman, Belgian, Swede, or Australian is as keen to make the CPC as his colleague in New York, Chicago, or San Francisco. The NCR spirit is as international as the sale of NCR machines.

There was an inspiring demonstration of this spirit in 1938 when the NCR managers convention was held in London with Colonel Deeds and Allyn in attendance. It was, in reality, a League of Nations dedicated to the purpose of making business procedure more efficient. There were representatives from Argentina, Brazil, Australia, South Africa, New Zealand, Dutch East Indies, India, Germany, Japan, France, Sweden, Switzerland, Holland, Denmark, Italy, Belgium, Austria, Czecho-Slovakia, Norway, Hungary, Finland, Rumania, and Egypt. The Foreign Department was organized as a branch of the Sales Department in June 1902. A few months later it was made into a separate entity. We can now take a look at the scheme of organization with its thirty-four subsidiaries and branches that serve practically all countries.

The entire NCR selling organization is divided into seven sections, the First comprising the United States and Canada. In the Second Section are Argentina, Bolivia, Brazil, Chile, Paraguay, Peru, and Uruguay. The Third embraces Australia, India, Guam, the Dutch East Indies, New Zealand, and the Philippines. Included in the Fourth are Belgium, Bulgaria, France, Germany, Denmark, Greece, Hungary, Italy, Holland, Norway, Poland, Portugal, Rumania, Russia, Spain, Sweden, Switzerland, Turkey, the Baltic States, Jugoslavia, Finland, and eight smaller countries. Constituting the Fifth are Great Britain, British West Africa, Egypt, South Africa, Palestine, Syria, Sierre Leone, Liberia, and Nigeria. The countries in the Sixth Section are Mexico, Cuba, Colombia, Bermuda, the Dutch West Indies, Jamaica, French West Indies, and the remaining Latin American republics not in the Second Section. China and Japan are the most important members of the Seventh Section which also takes in French Indo-China, the Straits Settlements, the Federated Malay States, and Thailand.

London is the headquarters of the foreign field. Here, in a company-owned building, George A. Marshall, Vice President Overseas Sales, keeps his fingers on the pulse of the globe-girdling organization of which he is head. In him you have the embodiment of another NCR success story. Born in Ontario, Canada, his first occupation was as school teacher. With the outbreak of the First World War he joined the colors serving as machine gunner in the Canadian Army. With peace he became a life insurance agent in Denver. Later he returned to Canada and cast about for a job. An opportunity to become agent for an American business machine firm developed. The post, however, was not to be available for three weeks.

In the meantime he met an old friend on the street in Toronto. When he asked him what he was doing he replied that he was selling NCR cash registers, adding: "Why don't you have a try at it?" Marshall answered: "I have three weeks of idle time ahead of me. I will take your advice." In 1920 he became a salesman in the Toronto office at $35 a week. He forgot about the prospective job because he has been with the Company ever since.

From the beginning Marshall showed the stuff that has enabled him to rise to high place. He developed into a crack salesman and also displayed marked executive ability. One night he received a telegram from Dayton stating that he had been made Acting Manager for Cuba. Between darkness and dawn he was pitch-forked from a salesman's job in Toronto to an important executive post in a foreign country. He was ignorant of the Spanish language and knew nothing of Spanish business procedure. He took over and made good on the Cuban assignment, starting his climb upward and onward.

Adaptability to alien environment, together with his unusual executive capacity, marked Marshall for larger overseas service. Late in 1928 he was appointed Assistant Manager of the British organization. In this post he had supervision of Sales Agents, District Instructors, Conventions, Sales Promotion, Sales School, Show Rooms, and Advertising. The next year saw him Manager for Great Britain. In 1933 he was designated Vice President in charge of Overseas Sales.

Vision and foresight are among the outstanding Marshall assets. At the time of the Munich Conference fiasco he realized that war was inevitable. He sent a form letter to all European managers warning them of the imminence of conflict and urging precautions in the shape of duplicate records, abundance of cash, emergency budgets, ample stocks of parts, and understudies for skilled staffs.

When the impact of war came in 1939 Marshall's precautions aided the Company to carry on. As was the case on the Continent, in and out of the zone of war, old registers were bought and reconditioned. Stock rather than sales had priority. In England women were trained to supplant the repair men who

went into the armed services. With the taking over
of the NCR repair and assembly plant by the British
government for munitions manufacture Marshall
saw to it that his old staff was retained. Thus he
kept his mechanical force intact to become available
for NCR work when normal conditions returned.

Another precaution was the leasing of a country
house twenty miles from London which was set up
as alternative headquarters in the event that the
London offices were destroyed. Duplicate records
were kept here during the war. It became a refuge
for personnel and their families whose houses had
been bombed, and was also used as a convalescent
home for bomb-injured personnel just out of hospital.
Following the end of the European conflict the
Vache, as it was called, became a temporary residential training school for apprentice mechanics.

The NCR spirit of family co-operation and support was never more evident than in Europe during
and after the war. While the conflict raged 75 children of members of the staff in France were temporarily adopted by some of the Swiss personnel.
Everywhere the NCR organization worked as a unit
to alleviate suffering and to keep the Company flag
flying.

To return to the expansion of the overseas organization, Patterson was an advocate of on-the-spot
production wherever possible. For one thing it
expedited distribution. Then, too, the employment
of native workers made for good will for the product.

Moreover, the branch NCR factory became part and parcel of the industry of the country contributing to its economic prestige and advancement.

The first NCR overseas plant was built in 1903 in *Alte Jacobstrasse*, Berlin. It was granted the right to manufacture NCR cash registers and to use all patents in Europe. Business expanded so rapidly that it became necessary to move to a larger factory in 1911. Eleven years later the plant at *Werra und Thiemannstrasse, Neukölln*, was erected. It housed the executive offices as well as the factory. Like all other NCR branch plants, it was a replica of the Dayton factory in that it was a daylight structure. Windows took up the major part of the wall space. When the Second World War crashed the German subsidiary operated under the title of *National-Krupp Registrier Kassen G.m.b.h.* This resulted from the merger, negotiated by Colonel Deeds, of the National and Krupp business machine interests.

The NCR business in Japan began in 1897 with general agents. As the years progressed a Japanese company—*Nippon Kinsen Torokuki Kabushiki Kaisha*—was organized by the Fujiyama family. In 1935 Colonel Deeds went to Japan and effected an arrangement by which NCR acquired 70 per cent of the stock of the Japanese company. The Japanese plant was sold on January 27th, 1940.

Since Great Britain was the first NCR overseas outpost and because it is the headquarters of the foreign field, it may be well to trace the company expansion there. From a one-room store in London's Strand in 1886 with a single employee the Company has extended to 86 branches well distributed over the entire United Kingdom. More than 1000 persons were on the payroll when the Second World War began. Of this force 400 were mechanics engaged in service work for users.

In no other domain, with the possible exception of France, did the NCR cash register encounter greater resistance at the start than in Britain. The British are a conservative people steeped in traditions of the old ways of doing things. Business habits, like titles, passed from father to son. The handwritten record ruled in banking and business. There was also the deep-rooted insular prejudice against so-called "Yankee inventions." The cash register, with its speed and efficiency, was a distinct innovation. In the early days it was almost regarded as an intruder. Salesmanship and service won out against the stoutest conservative diehards wedded to tradition. National machines became part of the commercial and banking order in Britain.

The chronology of the Company's London quarters tells the story of progress. In 1904, after successive moves to increasingly larger quarters, the NCR took over a big building in Tottenham Court Road and an adjoining one in Store Street. It now occupied an entire city block. Here, as in the United States and elsewhere, attractive window displays were features. In 1937 the Company dedicated its present imposing building—one of the finest commercial structures in England—in Marylebone Road. It contains over 110,000 square feet, four times the floor space of the old premises in Tottenham Court Road. The dedication was a distinguished occasion. The Earl of Denbigh, senior director of the English company, was chairman. The manager of the Fifth Section, D.A.F. Donald, outlined the history of the company. The building was formally opened by The Rt. Hon. Reginald Mc-Kenna, one of Britain's foremost bankers and a former wartime Chancellor of the Exchequer.

After nearly sixty years of proved service the National cash register is an accepted aid to British business. When the war absorbed so many men on repair service their places were taken by teen age boys in uniform. These boys not only serviced the registers but also sold supplies. They became a link between client and company. Frequently they tip off salesmen for prospects. Some have risen to be salesmen via the sales school.

When the NCR began to produce accounting machines a fertile, if difficult, field for expansion opened up in Britain. It was difficult because of the ingrained conservatism, nowhere more pronounced than in banking. The cash register had pointed the way to mechanization of retail business operations. The merchant, therefore, was cash register minded. A vast amount of spade work was required to "sell" banks, government offices and institutions, and big corporations.

The introduction of NCR accounting machines precipitated something of a revolution in the British organization. It was necessary to educate the Sales Force in the technique of mechanized accounting, to teach the mechanical staff to deal with a new and different type of product, and to open schools for the training of operators. It involved a considerable amount of adjustment. The process of adjustment, however, did not apply exclusively to the NCR organization. The British corporate and banking mind also required a degree of adjustment to the new mechanized order.

The campaign started with the Class 2000. British municipalities purchased them for control and analysis of incoming revenue. Various British concerns had developed what they call "hire-purchase," that is, installment buying, on a large scale. The initial installation for posting this type of business was in Harrods, one of London's greatest department stores where it proved to be a complete success. The next field to be entered was commercial ledger posting. The first order was from Thos. Cook & Son, famed as the world's largest travel agency. These installations were the forerunners of what became a constantly expanding business in accounting machines.

With the acquisition of the Ellis Adding Typewriter Company by NCR and the development of the Class 3000 new vistas of British business opened.

One of the earliest successes was in the decision of
Lloyds Bank, Limited to proceed with the mechanization of its branch accounting. To understand just
what this meant it is necessary to know something
about the organization of the large London commercial banks. Lloyds is one of the so-called Big Five,
the other four being the Midland, Limited; West-
minster, Limited; Barclays Limited, and National
Provincial, Limited. Each employs a staff of not less
than 10,000 people. They have branches in all towns
and villages of any size throughout the kingdom. It is
not uncommon for one of the Big Five to have 500
branches. Three of the Big Five use Nationals for
normal routine work. Machines are also installed
in the other two.

One of the picturesque features of London finance
is the old private banking house. They have resisted
the inroads of amalgamation with large banks and
retain, in more than one instance, century-old traditions. Between them they divide the cream of
private, as distinct from commercial, banking business. The list of their clients is like a replica of pages
from Burke's Peerage. Some of these private banks,
such as the Rothchilds, for example, are linked with
events that made world history.

It was Nathan Rothchild who broke the news of
the victory at Waterloo to the British government in
an adventure that has become a legend. He anticipated the defeat of Napoleon, was stationed at a
small town on the Belgian coast, and had a boat

ready. The moment he heard the great news he put
out for England in the midst of a great storm that
nearly engulfed him. The Rothchilds still occupy
the premises in St. Swithin's Lane in London's City
—the financial district—where Nathan had his office.
When I visited Lord Rothchild some years ago I
was shown this room which is exactly as its most
famous occupant left it. On the desk was his quill
pen and the sand shaker he used to blot his signature.
With sentimental traditions like this it is not surprising that the London private banks represent the last
word in conservatism. Yet more than two score of
them use National bookkeeping machines.

Unique among the financial institutions of the
world is the Bank of England—the Old Lady of
Thread-needle Street—with its 250 years of service.
It is Britain's Bank of Banks. In addition to being
the government bank "The Bank," as it is familiarly
called in London, handles note issues and loans and
also acts as banker for each of the large commercial
banks. It has the largest dividend-issuing department of any institution in the world. Today this
citadel of conservatism resounds with the click of
National accounting machines which are used for
general columnar work of all types. National accounting machines are in various British government
services including the Post Office Savings Banks, the
War Office and the Air Ministry, to say nothing of
stock-brokers' offices, factories and warehouses.

The growth of the NCR accounting machine

business in Britain is evident in a comparison of sales over a nine year period. In this time the business increased five fold. Britain has found the mechanized way.

The Overseas organization has made important contributions to the engineering side of the business. The development of the Class 3000 from a 4 to a 6 total machine was designed in Switzerland. The adaptation of the same machine to Indian currency came from Berlin. The (16) printer of the Class 6000 enabling each operating key to be used at will for either single or multiple operations, was designed by a British mechanic. In some countries no loose-leaf system may be used for legal documents. A bound book must be employed. The Swiss Accounting Machine Division invented a carriage which enables the Class 3000 to do this.

The success of the Company abroad, as at home, has been due to the contributions of innumerable individuals who, in a relatively brief chronicle such as the present volume, must be nameless. One outstanding contribution, however, should be cited. It was the introduction of Budget Control by Ernest F. Jones. As a very young man he was employed as stenographer to John H. Patterson during the latter's management of the English company. He became successively secretary to the European Advisory Committee, Secretary of the British Company, Financial Director for Europe, and was Financial

Comptroller of Overseas Business at his untimely death in 1939.

Stories of resource stud the records of the overseas selling force. Nowhere did the early salesmen encounter greater handicaps in covering their territory than in Australia. Its vast distances, limited railway facilities, and widely separated communities made travel a serious problem not unmixed with hazard. Salesmen were compelled to use horse, and later motor, transport. Often their vehicles were overturned in rushing streams; frequently they were marooned in the bush for days. Mishaps of this kind were so common that many salesmen carried camping outfits and slept in the open.

Stories of ambitious young men who made good as NCR salesmen know no geographical lines as this one attests: At one time two stores stood side by side in Sydney. One was a big suburban department store employing many assistants; the other was a small cake shop run by the proprietor who baked the cakes which were sold over the counter by a young girl. The total weekly turnover of the shop was $300. When the owner of the department store met the baker he treated him with condescension.

The baker was young. He yearned to be a salesman. In its insistent search for new and promising material for the selling force the NCR came in contact with him. He persuaded the National representative to give him a chance. Within a year he had not only developed into a first class salesman but found himself, one day, sitting in the office of his one-time department store neighbor arranging for a survey of the establishment and its methods. At the conclusion of the survey he sold the proprietor $15,000 worth of cash registers.

The Hundred Point Club and Sales Contests play their part in inspiring enthusiasm and friendly rivalry in Australia, as elsewhere in the foreign field. The Australian is keen on teams. Often he will do more for a team than for himself. To stimulate sales competition three teams were organized, one for Sydney, a second for Melbourne, and the third for the rest of the country. A banner was offered for the team that rolled up the best selling record each year. It was held by the winning team until another captured it. After twelve contests the banner was hung in the convention room in NCR headquarters in Sydney. The new banner, presented to the Australian NCR by the British NCR organization is the flag that flew over the Company offices in London during the blitz.

An Australian salesman once defined the NCR in effective fashion. This is what he said:

"The NCR is the hardest business in the world to get into because it sets such a high standard for its applicants. It knows that it offers opportunities and expects a man to fight to get his chance to seize these opportunities. It is the hardest business in the world to stay in because a man is judged by results. He cannot stay by influence or by offering alibis. On the other hand it is the hardest business in the world to get out of because the NCR is so constituted that if it feels a man has in him the makings for success, despite a temporary lack of results, it will not let him go so long as it is felt that there is a chance to bring out the latent talents believed to be in him."

Like Australia, India with her teeming millions offered difficulties for NCR penetration, but for a different reason. One lay in the character of the currency. A rupee, which corresponds in value to 33 cents in American money, is subdivided into 16 annas of 12 pies each. This peculiarity, which has no parallel in any other country, made India a difficult market for the manufacturer of calculating machines. Another handicap was the small size of the average shop which is often an open stall along a lane or in a bazaar.

The NCR surmounted the principal difficulty and brought out a line of cash registers for Indian currency. In the beginning they went mainly into the foreign-owned shops. Subsequently they found their way into dairies and cafes. National registers ring up sales in many picturesque Indian places none more impressive than in Darjeeling which is 8500 feet above sea level within view of the majestic Himalayas dominated by Mt. Everest, highest mountain in the world and still unconquered by man. One interesting fact is that all registers in India are operated by natives. This is because the ratio of population is 500 Indians to one European. Prac-

tically all work is done by Indians. With the introduction of the Class 3000 the field of operations in
India widened to include mechanized accounting in
mills, factories, ports, municipalities, railroads, and
telegraph offices.

The pioneer NCR salesmen had their baptisms of
fire and flood. One experience of Johan Sande in
Norway will illustrate how emergencies were met
and overcome. The episode occurred in 1901.

Sande's elder brother was an NCR salesman whom
he had coached in the study of the Primer. Young
Sande became so interested in the technique of NCR
salesmanship that he decided to try to get a job with
the Company himself. When he approached N. E.
Frykholm, then principal NCR representative in
Norway, he was told that he was too young. Sande
was so persistent that he was taken on and sent on a
trial trip. He returned with two orders for high
grade machines, an excellent result in those days.
He got the job.

Sande was first sent to the far north of Norway
where travelling was difficult. Storms, bitter cold,
and winter darkness impeded progress. Added to
this was the absence of cash register minded merchants. Most of them had never heard of a cash
register. It was therefore necessary for salesmen to
carry sample machines for demonstration. Many
small towns in northern Norway were without quays
which meant that luggage and samples had to be
brought ashore in row boats.

One night Sande was due to land in a small town
to demonstrate his register to a very difficult prospect. It was highly important that this man be sold.
If he bought, others in the community would follow
his example because he was a leading citizen. As ill
luck would have it, the sample machine fell into the
water a few minutes after it was loaded in the row
boat. With great effort it was hauled out and con-
veyed to the town hotel. Both the machine and the
sample trunk were soaked with salt water. The demonstration was scheduled for the next morning.

Now began a night of labor and anxiety for Sande.
He unscrewed the machine cabinet and started to
dry the interior of the register in front of the hotel
oven. By dawn this had been accomplished. Then
Sande noticed that the pasted indicator figures were
loose. Some were completely detached. This seemed
to be a catastrophe. The outlook appeared hopeless.
As he sat despairing Sande noticed a clipping from
an NCR bulletin pasted inside the lid of his sample
trunk. It reproduced a poem which began:

"If you strike a thorn or rose

Keep a-goin'."

These lines stirred Sande to renewed action. He
procured glue and pasted on the indicator figures
after which he oiled the machine. It was now ready
to be shown at the hour fixed for the demonstration.
The prospect was of the dour and grouchy type not
uncommon in that part of Norway. He would never
buy anything at first sight. After Sande had made his

demonstration the merchant left the hotel room with a curt "not to-day." To Sande this was the final blow after his long, sleepless, and laborious night. While he brooded dejectedly the door opened and the merchant, now amiable and smiling, said:

"Well, young man, I like your way of demonstrating. Let me have two of your registers."

When Johan Sande died in 1942 he had been an NCR salesman for forty-one years. He was an honored member of the NCR Old Guard that represented a valiant tradition of service.

Not all the experiences of NCR men in remote places were marked by stress and strain. Some had the element of humor. This is what happened to an executive who went to Argentina:

When he arrived in Buenos Aires the executive informed the local manager that he was not going to gauge Argentina by the gay and beautiful capital city. He was determined to go back country where travelling was not easy. Furthermore, he did not want to be accompanied by the manager but only by an employee who would act as interpreter. The manager decided to send him to Tucumen which meant a long and tiresome journey, part of it through a desert. Accompanied by the manager's secretary the executive set out.

As they approached the desert the secretary informed his companion that the dust and dirt would be so intense that it would be necessary to close all the windows in the train compartment. When this was done the atmosphere became almost stifling. To escape suffocation and as a protection against germs the secretary further advised the executive to wrap a handkerchief soaked with peroxide of hydrogen around his face. Having taken this precaution the man from Dayton went to bed.

One of the personal adornments of the executive was a large brown moustache of which he was inordinately proud. When he woke up the next morning he found to his horror that the peroxide had turned his moustache into part brown and part white. There was nothing for him to do but to sacrifice it.

Finally, there is the story of Albert Moth, a little epic of courage, character, and loyalty. Moth began his career with the Company when he was eighteen as stenographer to the British Sales Manager. From the start he was ambitious to become a salesman fretting because he was told that he was too young to join the sales force. His chance came when the NCR in Spain asked for an English correspondent. Moth was given the post. With the outbreak of the Spanish Civil War he began to display the capacity and resource that were henceforth to distinguish him. With Madrid under siege a number of families of employees whose homes had been destroyed by enemy action were forced to live in the cellar of the Company building. When Marshall inspected the scene he decided that the families should be removed to safety. Moth was charged with the task of evacuation. He settled the dependents in a hotel in Manosque, France which the Company took over.

Moth was not content to remain in France. His heart was in Spain. He persuaded the London office to send him back to Spain which involved a difficult and hazardous undertaking. He had left ten agents in Spain; he found three on his return. The country was rent with civil strife; the NCR business was deranged; cash registers for sale had vanished. Moth was determined to restore the NCR organization despite all these obstacles and succeeded. The building of a virtually new business without stock, capital, or experience in selling and management in a country torn by war is one of the outstanding NCR romances of achievement.

Moth combed Spain for registers and found a few. All needed overhauling. He started a service department and made them saleable. Thirty Dayton machines had arrived at Santander just before the civil war broke out and were held in the custom house there. Since they belonged to the Spanish NCR subsidiary which had headquarters in Madrid they were nominally enemy property and confiscated. Moth got them out.

More than once Moth acquired used registers in unconventional fashion. The equipment of a bar at Valladoloid was put up for sale. The owner would not sell his cash register which he regarded as his most valuable asset. Moth purchased all the bar fixtures and ultimately managed to buy the register. He made a profit on the sale of all the other stuff and on the register as well.

Barely a year after he took over in Spain Moth had twelve agents. Two made the CPC. By the end of 1938 his organization reached its quota month after month. There were now fourteen agencies and three service depots. During this period almost the only help he got from the Company was moral support. When the Civil War ended in 1939 Moth entered the capital on a truck loaded with potatoes. He took over the Madrid office and operated it as manager. The Company's fine premises in the Gran Via had been destroyed by shell fire so Moth secured another property, installed offices and a service department and began a profitable operation.

With the outbreak of the Second World War Moth cabled London that he desired to enter military service. Persuaded to continue with the Company until the British Government could use his services or his class called, he carried on in Spain. After the German break-through at Sedan in May 1940 Moth renewed his request to join up. This time there could be no denial.

Once more he faced and vanquished obstacles. He wanted to become a R.A.F. pilot. His age—he was now 29—and the fact that his wife was of foreign birth, were against him. Finally he was accepted for ground defense and drafted for training as a machine gunner. After passing a practically perfect examination he applied to the R.A.F. Selection Board for training as a pilot, but was turned down. He tried again and was accepted. With only an elementary education he qualified as Sergeant Observer in the Bomber Command and was posted to a Manchester Squadron. His first operational flight was on the night of June 5th, 1942. He never returned. His plane was shot down by anti-aircraft fire over the Loire River in France.

The benediction on Moth's gallant life and death is best pronounced in the closing paragraph of the NCR booklet which tells his story. It says:

"His story will be forgotten soon except perhaps as a tale told to, or by, his sons. But whilst we who knew him live, he cannot die. He lives on in our memories, a reproach and an inspiration. A reproach because, with perhaps ampler opportunities, ours is so poor a record. An inspiration, revealing what courage, resolution, and devotion to duty can achieve."

The achievement of Albert Moth puts the capstone on the NCR overseas structure. As in the home edifice, it has been reared with faith in the product, unswerving loyalty, and an abiding sense of service to Company and client.

CHAPTER X

Humanizing Employee Relations

IT IS altogether fitting that the NCR factory where welfare for industry had its birth should exemplify its highest tradition and provide a model for the world of production. Generally regarded today as a vital contribution to successful employee relations, welfare owes its inception to John H. Patterson. As was the case with so many of the innovations that he initiated, he flouted the established order when first he brought light, comfort, and convenience to the domain of his workers.

In view of working conditions as we know them today it is difficult to realize that a bare half century ago the average American factory was dark, dingy, and in the main unsanitary. Hot meals served in dining halls were undreamed of. Labor was drudgery unrelieved by the human or the humane touch. The worker was a cog in the industrial machine.

When Patterson saw one of his women workers heating a pot of coffee on a radiator and got the inspiration to install facilities for hot food for his women employees, he set a precedent. This was the beginning of welfare in American industry. When hot meals were served for women in dining rooms the second step was taken in what became progressively a complete transformation of factory working conditions at NCR.

Patterson's fellow industrialists thought that all this was little short of fantastic. They said to him: "Why pamper your employees? Altruism has no place in a factory." There was nothing altruistic about Patterson's idea nor was there any pampering. His philosophy of welfare, like his philosophy of production and selling, was eminently practical. The welfare program, as he projected it, was simply good business. It paid increasing dividends in better workmanship, better product, and made for that great objective of industry which is content in work.

Industrialists who derided the NCR welfare program after it was well under way declared: "We can't afford it. Besides, we would rather put the money into the pay envelope." They did not realize that the cost of welfare, even on the scale practiced at the NCR, is too low to affect the pay envelope materially. Welfare activities cost the Company $107 per employee per year, or a trifle over $2 a week. Rarely does so little produce so much in service and satisfaction.

You will recall that early in Patterson's industrial career a shipment of $50,000 worth of cash registers was returned because of mechanical defects and, following this costly episode, he moved his desk into the factory. Living elbow to elbow with his workers he discovered that there was a rapid turnover of skilled workmen without apparent reason, that the plant was dingy, unsightly, and unsanitary, that light and ventilation were poor, that lack of safety features on dangerous machinery caused frequent injuries, and that the workmen were indifferent and insubordinate.

Patterson discovered something else that was to influence his outlook and shape his attitude towards labor. It was the realization that the three basic factors for success in industrial management are Methods, Materials and Men. He further realized that in the early conduct of his factory he had overlooked the all-important element of Men. He could buy the first two elements—Methods and Materials—but he could not buy the most essential which is Men. The relationship with them had to be created. This is precisely what Patterson did, laying the cornerstone of present-day NCR management.

Patterson's welfare scheme developed into two general sections. One was the improvement of working conditions in the factory; the other was education and recreation for employees and their families. In the second phase of the program was the raw material for the making of better citizens and the general uplift of the community.

When Patterson began to improve working conditions he started a peaceful industrial revolution. He was among the first employers to install safety devices. He introduced bathrooms which the employees could use on factory time, individual lockers, rest rooms, first aid stations, schools for apprentices, and a complete medical department with doctors, nurses, masseurs, and later X-ray equipment and a dental clinic. Visiting nurses cared for the families of the workers. Thus welfare began to take on a broader community scope.

Remembering the darkness and dinginess of the first small factory that he acquired when he embarked in the cash register business in 1884 Patterson made a notable contribution to industry which fitted into his welfare pattern. "Let there be light" became his abiding maxim when the time came for him to build a plant. He told the architects that he wanted the walls to be 80 per cent glass. They replied that it was impossible. Patterson did not know the mean-of the word "impossible." He had his way with the result that NCR had the first so-called "daylight" factory in the United States.

With his passion for cleanliness Patterson installed a laundry to provide fresh towels, napkins, table-cloths, sleevelets, and aprons for the factory workers. They are washed without cost to the personnel. As a special service on wet days umbrellas are now supplied free of charge.

Most industrialists would have been happy with the factory changes that had been introduced and the content and efficiency that followed. Patterson's vision encompassed much more. Having achieved a transformation inside the factory he set to work to accomplish one outside the walls. In those days—it was in 1884—the approaches to most factories were littered with rubbish, packing cases, empty barrels, and scraps of metal. It made an unsightly mess. Patterson determined to do away with it. He engaged the services of a well-known firm of landscape engineers in Brookline, Mass., and the beautification of the factory grounds began. Shrubbery, trees, flowers and lawns were planted and window boxes installed. The plant lost a great deal of its "factory" appearance. It led Patterson to say: "The product of a factory is no better than the lawn outside."

The NCR factory was located in a part of Dayton called Slidertown. It was said in the city that "everything bad in Dayton slid down to Slidertown." Nor did the name belie the neighborhood. It was a jungle of shacks, vacant lots strewn with tin cans, and the debris often seen in the environs of big cities. Tramps and criminals infested the shacks and became a menace to women as they came and went to work. With all its beautification the NCR plant stood out as a bright oasis in the desert of Slidertown rubbish.

There was another evil. The boys of the neighborhood were as rough and tumble as the area in which they lived. They smashed factory windows and endangered other NCR property.

Patterson felt that these youngsters were not inherently bad and that they were mainly bent on mischief. Idleness contributed largely to their delinquency. He felt, too, that they had the makings of good citizens if they were put to some congenial work. Now was evolved an aspect of the welfare plan which developed into a nationwide movement.

Always a believer in utility, Patterson conceived the idea of having the Slidertown boys start gardens. He allotted a plot of ground to each boy, gave him seed and tools, and engaged a competent gardener as instructor. He offered prizes for the best gardens thereby stimulating interest and competition. Before long the one-time neighborhood pests became so absorbed in their gardens that they forgot to smash windows and get into other mischief. Soon they had a garden club. These gardens marked the beginning of the children's garden movement with its redemption of backyards and vacant lots throughout the United States. Today no progressive school department is without its school gardens. Many cities have garden associations.

Patterson found a more permanent and profitable task for his juvenile proteges. He started them on making box furniture, again providing tools, material, and an instructor. The boys responded as eagerly to the new work as they had gone in for gardening. With these two activities Patterson found the best possible cure for idleness and mischief.

In 1912 the Boys Box Furniture Company was organized to engage the boys during the winter months after school hours, and on Saturdays. They were obliged to qualify as gardeners before they could enjoy the benefits of the furniture company.

Scrap wood from the factory was converted into useful articles of furniture and sold to the public. Through the operation of the furniture company the boys learned business methods. Many successful NCR employees were boy gardeners and box furniture makers in their youth.

Now began what became a pretentious neighborhood welfare program. Patterson established the House of Usefulness which was put in charge of Mrs. Lena Harvey Tracy, a noted city social settlement worker. Here the neighborhood boys were given the opportunity to learn clay modelling, wood carving, and drawing. Then Patterson gave the girls something to do. They were taught sewing, embroidering, and cooking. The entire juvenile population in the area adjacent to the factory buzzed with useful effort.

The example of the boys and girls inspired their parents to bestir themselves. Patterson endowed a school for landscape gardening and offered prizes for the most beautiful lawns and backyards. People vied with each other to beautify their surroundings, and provide a pleasant environment for the man of the family when he came home after work. Slidertown became South Park, a desirable residential community, with an Improvement Association.

As part of his neighborhood welfare scheme Patterson inaugurated Saturday morning entertainments for children in the NCR auditorium. They were shown educational films, heard good music, witnessed pageants, and received a treat of fruit and cake. There was sound reasoning behind those Saturday morning entertainments. The children who attended, as well as their older sisters and brothers, were the NCR workers of tomorrow.

Early Patterson encouraged visits to the factory by members of the employees' families. The youngster wanted "to see where daddy works." At a plastic age they got the feel of what the NCR meant. When they joined the ranks of workers they were no strangers to the factory.

Neighborhood welfare touched nearly every detail of home life, influencing NCR workers and others as well. As far back as the mid-nineties Patterson had established a Domestic Economy School to teach housekeeping to the girls of the community. Soon thereafter a kindergarten came into being followed by a Mothers' Guild. Thus young and old came within the scope of an educational work that instilled self-respect and made for adequate preparedness for the responsibilities of life and labor.

Soon after the turn of the century the Rubicon Club—named after the old Patterson farm—was organized in a building near the factory. The membership was drawn from factory workers as well as other people in the neighborhood. The club became the rallying point for the entire community. A boys club, an offshoot of the Rubicon, had a printing shop and issued a monthly newspaper. Another adjunct was the Women's Club which devoted much time to betterment work, holding all-day sewings to make clothing for motherless children and for hospitals.

One consequence of all these activities—another evidence of the larger influence of factory welfare—was the organization of the Men's Welfare League by NCR men. It took over two neighborhood social settlements and conducted classes in sewing, basketry, wood carving, water colors, physical development, and dancing for men, women, and children. Two military companies were formed for neighborhood boys. A vocational school was maintained for 200 people. Free public baths, the first in Dayton, were thrown open to the community. In 1906 the Men's Welfare League conducted a cooperative vacation trip for 1700 NCR factory employees to Port Huron, Michigan, where the vacationists lived in tents. The NCR provided the food.

The NCR had originated the educational trip idea as early as 1893 when it sponsored the journey of a group of employees to the Chicago World's Fair. At intervals foremen and workmen were sent on trips to get new ideas on manufacturing and working conditions. In 1904 the Company paid part, and in some cases all, the travelling expenses of hundreds of employees to the St. Louis World's Fair. These trips were in line with Patterson's fundamental idea of education. He believed that travel was a great broadener of outlook. This policy has been continued. Department heads, foremen, job foremen, and factory workers are sent on trips to attend meet-

ings of various organizations and to get the benefits
of safety conventions.

Patterson always encouraged meetings of employees because he felt that through interchange of
ideas their interest and efficiency were increased.
What began as a regular Friday morning meeting of
heads of departments, supervisors, and foremen developed into the Advance Club which discussed common problems of production and company policies.
The Advance Club became the Progress Club of today composed of so-called ABC employees, that is,
employees above the bench workers.

At this point it is well to keep in mind the fact that
as Patterson widened his welfare program he had
no precedents to guide him. He had planted his
original idea in a virgin field. Every phase of its
expansion made a contribution to factory betterment,
not only at the NCR, but eventually to industry
everywhere.

Patterson was quick to grasp a new idea and capitalize it. On a trip to New York in 1901 he saw his
first motion picture. Previously he had used stere-
opticon slides to illustrate his lectures at conventions
and factory meetings. The moment he saw moving
pictures he determined to adapt them for NCR purposes. He arranged with the Biograph Company,
one of the pioneer film concerns, to make 6000 feet of
motion picture film at the factory. It was the first
time that animated pictures were used by any industry. With one of the original Edison projectors,

Patterson showed the factory film in his so-called Factory Talk—the story of NCR welfare—which he gave throughout the United States and abroad.

In 1910 Joseph Urban produced the first motion picture in color in England with the presentation of the Durbar in India. The process was then called Kinemacolor. When Patterson saw the Durbar in London he began to use Kinemacolor for the factory films. The reproduction of the employees' gardens in color was particularly effective. At one time Patterson had three sets of the factory films in Kinemacolor touring the country.

Patterson's pet theory of teaching through the eye led to another innovation in factory welfare. It began when he inaugurated noon hour entertainment for employees in what was then known as Welfare Hall. At first he put on educational slides and had prominent men and women talk on current events. The workers did not seem to care for this kind of diversion. They wanted entertainment so Patterson gave it to them by introducing motion pictures. Today the big auditorium is filled at noon with employees who watch the latest movies as they eat their lunches which they bring from home or buy at cost in the various commissaries in the auditorium. Thirteen miles of film are shown each week at the noon hour entertainment.

Patterson was a firm believer in fitness of body as a necessary requisite for the worker. He put "Health Hints" and "Keep Fit" departments in all the early

NCR house publications. Moreover he practiced what he preached. Two of the most valuable features of NCR welfare, therefore, are exercise and recreation in non-working hours. In 1894 girl employees were given calisthenics. Two years later the company fitted up a gymnasium at the Patterson Grade School. It was open to the NCR personnel. Soon came NCR gun clubs for trap-shooting, base-ball, basket ball, and bowling teams.

The NCR recreation program got under way in 1904 when Patterson made part of his beautifully wooded estate, Hills and Dales, available for factory employees. Roads were built, picnic shelters and fireplaces set up, and a golf course laid out. There were also facilities for band concerts, baseball, dancing and tennis, as well as a children's playground. In 1910 the NCR Club for foremen, heads of departments, assistants and their families was opened in Hills and Dales without expense to the members. With this began what is known as industrial recreation.

In 1937, at the instigation of Colonel Deeds, development work was started on a 226 acre tract of woodland within sight of the factory buildings. Two years afterward Old River, one of the finest recreation centers in the country, was opened for the exclusive use of NCR employees, their families, and their friends. Old River, which takes its name from the fact that the old river channel of the Miami once ran through the tract, is equipped with all picnic and recreational facilities including one of the largest swimming pools in the Middle West. There is a lagoon, one and a half miles in length, with canoes and row boats always available for the recreationists. To relieve parents of the responsibility of entertaining their small children a "Tot Lot For Kiddies" provides wading pools, swings, a merry-go-round, and sand boxes. For those who do not wish to burden themselves with picnic lunches, hot suppers may be obtained in the shelter houses.

In winter the Coliseum at the Fair Grounds, which seats 3600 people, is rented by the Company for employee recreation purposes. Here departmental basket ball teams hold their games. Ping pong, bait casting, badminton, indoor archery, are also included in the winter activities. Once a month a party is given so that the NCR families can get together for dancing and other forms of amusement.

Two factors underlie NCR industrial recreation. One is that it provides healthful diversion that increases worker efficiency; the other is that it creates and fosters the NCR family spirit.

To fitness of body Patterson linked fitness of mind. For him continuous education was a "must" in the code of life and work. He constantly emphasized the value of training as a stimulus to ambition and advancement. In the formative years of the Company the educational facilities were more or less scattered. The night school for so-called Owl Classes were started in 1903 in a room at the factory. The first class studied methods of selling cash registers. The course was expanded to include salesmanship, advertising, shop mathematics, public speaking, mechanical drawing, accounting, printing, Spanish, blueprint reading, home economics, and dressmaking. Through the night classes more than one NCR worker has emancipated himself from tool and bench and joined the selling force or assumed an executive position.

Evening classes—the name OWL was abandoned sometime ago—are held under the auspices of the Educational Department during the fall and winter months for all employees who wish to join. They run for a period of twenty-six weeks. The only charge is a registration fee of $1. For 1944-5 the course embraced blueprint reading, mathematics, mechanical drawing, tool designing, general shop practice, machine shop training, bookkeeping, accounting, typewriting and shorthand. The NCR apprentice system covers tool-making, machining, model and pattern making, drafting, tool-designing, and printing. The Company also trains students of the Parker Cooperative High School of Dayton and recognized cooperative universities.

As you have already been told, Patterson's first venture in welfare was to enable his women workers to have hot food. In the succeeding years food has played an important part in welfare development. It is one of the many factors that have combined for content in work. The first modest kitchen and makeshift dining room have expanded to dimensions that would serve a small community. No industrial plant in the United States has more complete food facilities. The Horseshoe Room, where executives, heads of departments, supervisors and foremen lunch, has become an institution. The Junior Executive Club, organized in 1898, is maintained for job foremen and assistant heads of departments. There is a large employees cafeteria and also a Girls Dining Room. In addition, food is served in the foundry and power house. Food may also be obtained from the various stores scattered throughout the plant. In summer the factory commissary supplies the food for Sugar Camp and Old River. Prices in the NCR dining rooms are within the pocketbook of everyone.

Every facility to encourage thrift among employees, to safeguard their savings, and to give them economic security, is available. The NCR Employees Credit Union is typical of what is done. It makes loans at reasonable rates, thus protecting the workers from the exorbitant interest charges that prevail so often in outside agencies. The Union was established in 1937 by seven employees with a capital of $70. By 1945 the membership had grown to 6,000 with a capital of $1,115,000. During its operating period loans to members have totalled $3,500,000, the proceeds going for hospital and medical expenses, home improvement, purchase of automobiles, and furniture. It is a commentary on the character of NCR employees that the losses on money loaned have been approximately $2,900, or less than one tenth of one per cent of the entire amount loaned.

No less useful is the NCR Relief Association dating back to 1896, which provides sick and death benefits and medical service at low cost. It has a membership comprising 95 per cent of all the employees in the Dayton plant. A monthly payroll deduction for dues is permitted by the Company. This prevents members from becoming delinquent and assures continuous benefit. The Relief Association operates the refreshment stands and food wagons throughout the factory. The profits are turned into the general fund of the organization. The workers at the NCR share in group insurance and hospitalization. The ABC group of employees are enabled to make provision for an income after their retirement from active service through a contributory annuity plan.

Such is the span of NCR welfare. The benefits cannot be measured in terms of dollars and cents. The compensations, however, are invaluable. Welfare has contributed to a unique tradition of factory service. There are 1,461 members in the Twenty-Five Year Club. Of this number 710 have been with the company 25 to 30 years; 619 have been steadily employed from 30 to 40 years; 123 from 40 to 50 years, while 9 have rounded out more than 50 years. These records could not have been achieved without content in work which the humanizing of employee relations makes possible.

When Patterson extended his welfare work to the

boys and girls of Slidertown and their families he made the initial move in what became a drive for the betterment of Dayton. He realized that parks, boys clubs, and neighborhood improvement did not perform the bigger civic job. Dayton needed a strong dose of house cleaning. The city was ruled by politicians who, to employ a phrase once made by an eminent magazine writer, were "corrupt and contented." Public services were in a sad state of neglect; the school system lagged. Deep down Patterson felt that the NCR had a definite obligation to the community. Animated by this conviction he embarked on an adventure in community relations which bore rich fruit.

In the early summer of 1912 Patterson sent two men to New York to study civic conditions. He also sent a man to Europe to look into the technique of city government. The agents who went to New York discovered the Bureau of Municipal Research. The moment Patterson learned of its scope he decided that Dayton needed a similar set-up. Without delay he established a bureau to investigate city activities. Among other things the bureau published a pamphlet entitled "Government by Deficit" because Dayton finances were always in the red. This and kindred revelations began to waken the local citizenry to the fact that they were badly governed.

Patterson was first and last a business man. His experience as industrialist bred the conviction that a city should be run precisely like a corporation for the benefit of the citizens who are the stockholders. This meant clean government and confusion to the professional politicians. He saw in the City Manager Plan the realization of his ideal. Various small communities had tried it out with success. Under Patterson's direction a vigorous campaign of education for better government was launched by an organization largely effected and financed by him. Its objective was City Managership.

In the midst of this campaign the great flood broke with all its damage and disruption. What Patterson and his NCR associates did in that dark hour has already been told in these pages. The flood temporarily halted the civic campaign. It proved, however, to be an ill wind that blew good. The flood crisis welded public opinion for a change in city government because the municipal authorities had failed to meet the emergency with efficiency and resolution. The campaign for a City Manager was resumed with such vigor that when the time came for polling the people, by a large vote, adopted the plan. Dayton was the first large city to have a City Manager. Patterson was chairman of the commission that drew the City Charter. The plan went into effect January 1st, 1914 with Henry M. Waite as City Manager named by a charter commission of five members. The Bureau of Municipal Research became advisor to the new city government. Dayton had a rebirth of civic freedom.

In 1921 Patterson, together with members of his

family, financed and established the Dayton Foundation, which was instrumental in establishing vocational education in the public schools. It also sponsored various community humanitarian projects including the Neighborhood Improvement Association. Meanwhile the Bureau of Municipal Research was succeeded by the Dayton Research Association, the funds for which were supplied by the Dayton Foundation.

The NCR auditorium has a definite place in community affairs, and has become a center of civic activities. Originally the NCR School House, with a seating capacity of 520, it was rebuilt in 1922 to include a balcony and a large stage and seats for 2,300 persons. The auditorium is the scene of commencements of public and parochial schools and the University of Dayton, graduating exercises of hospital nurses, musical events, War Bond and Red Cross rallies, and patriotic meetings.

In September 1943 the NCR established the first Department of Community Relations in any American industrial concern to expand the discharge of its responsibility to the community. The Director is Wilbur M. Cotton who has had long experience in municipal management. One result was the organization of the Dayton District Development Committee, with Colonel Deeds as chairman. The Committee which has 165 members, has assumed general community leadership. Allyn is chairman of the Executive Committee. The Dayton District Development

Committee recognizes no race, creed, or color lines and includes representations of labor and management.

The purposes of the Dayton District Development Committee are fourfold. The first is the all-important task of veteran placement. Formerly the returned veteran seeking a job in Dayton had to deal with twelve different officially-designated agencies more or less scattered throughout the city. All the agencies were mobilized in a Veterans Information Center under one roof with the tangle of delay and red tape eliminated. The Center not only provides the necessary information but helps to secure jobs as well. The problem of retraining handicapped veterans also comes within its scope.

The second purpose of the Committee is to assist in the reconversion of Dayton industry from war to peacetime production with its myriad problems of contract termination and settlement, plant and equipment disposal, and inventories. Third is employment in industry, the idea being to stimulate commerce and industry to plan for higher levels of productive employment after the war. The fourth objective—community planning—involves long range projects for the development of the Dayton area. It supports a City Planning Board which controls the physical arrangement of the community so that it will function effectively and economically. This means proper zoning, the adequate deployment of streets, schools, bridges and public buildings, all to the end of achieving a harmonious civic picture.

The NCR contributed to the alleviation of the conditions that made Dayton a Number One Critical Labor Area during the high-powered production period of the second World War. Swollen by demands for labor which doubled the normal employment, plus a tremendous expansion of Army Air Force installations, Dayton was in a difficult situation. Accustomed to solving their own problems, the people of the city got together and formed an Emergency Committee of which Allyn was made Chairman. The Committee brought labor supply and demand into balance.

Behind the NCR's contribution to community betterment is a fundamental truth. A company, over a period of years, is no better than the community in which it is located. It is dependent upon its workers for their skill and their spirit which means its human relations. By helping to make the community a safer, healthier, and happier place to live in, the morale of employees is lifted, loyalty is inspired, and a more efficient product is the result.

CHAPTER XI

Men and Management

IN THE vast and inspiring panorama of American expansion the march of industry stands out
with peculiar impressiveness. Every segment is
aglow with cumulative development and the wizardry of mechanical progress. There was a time,
however, when personal or family ownership dominated the factory scene with the result that a degree
of paternalism influenced employee relations. The
worker asserted his individualism and was part of a
close-knit community of interests. In that other day
a man's skill was his social and economic security.
This was the time when plant and personnel were
relatively small.

Today, management has superseded personal and
family owership. Under the dynamic stimulus of
mass production the worker has lost his identity. No
one can question the worth or wisdom of mass output,
the hallmark of American industrial supremacy.
Mass output, however, has tended to bring about
mass personnel, the anonymity of the worker amid
the ceaseless flow of product. Industry has become
impersonal. The worker is inclined to look to the

Government for his social and economic security. Due to the sheer size of corporations the gap between top management and production has steadily widened. The ability of management and labor to work together has not kept pace with the advances in industry. It means that the major challenge to management is embodied in employee relations.

Half a century ago John H. Patterson began to meet this challenge when he moved his desk into the factory and worked shoulder to shoulder with his employees. Out of what became a close kinship he learned what was in their minds and hearts. It did not take him long to discover that industrial production was not only a mechanical process but the work of human beings with emotions and aspirations. Factory production was human production. Out of this realization has been reared the structure of NCR management policy. It is not the conventional man-to-man attitude. It is the larger conception that a factory is not only brick, stone, mortar and machinery but men and women as well. This is why the NCR is not a factory in the accepted sense but an institution; why the NCR spirit is not a mere phrase but a reality.

Some corporations grow so fast that individual importance, save at the top, shrinks with increasing expansion. The big task is to bind the employees into a team and at the same time maintain the integrity of individual power, initiative, and efficiency. This is what the NCR has achieved.

Checkers provide relaxation for factory workers during the recreation hour

Ping pong has its devotees at factory recess time

The Auditorium is a favorite spot for NCR employees where they enjoy the latest news and feature films during the noon hour: Here Bob Hope is entertaining them

Checkers provide relaxation for factory workers during the recreation hour

Ping pong has its devotees at factory recess time

The Auditorium is a favorite spot for NCR employees where they enjoy the latest news and feature films during the noon hour: Here Bob Hope is entertaining them

The Horseshoe Dining Room

Employees attend a departmental picnic at Old River

A conveniently located employees' cafeteria maintained by the Company serves hot food and beverages at minimum prices

Diversion on a hot day at Old River

To foster individualism Patterson pioneered Suggestion Contests which have proved over the years to be a definite factor in the establishment of congenial industrial relations. He conceived the idea for suggestions one morning when he found an old employee who had worked for him in the Jackson County coal field cleaning castings in the foundry. Surprised to find him doing this kind of work he asked him why he did not try to attract his foreman's attention and advance himself by suggesting some change that would improve a factory condition.

This conversation started a train of thought in Patterson. Suddenly he remembered something that he had heard in Venice a few years before. According to legend when a citizen of the republic of Venice wanted to call attention to an ill that needed correction he wrote out his criticism and dropped it in a slot in the wall of the Doge's Palace. This enabled the authorities to investigate the complaint without revealing the identity of the author.

When Patterson recalled this story he decided to adapt the principle to a factory suggestion system. Employees were asked to submit suggestions anonymously. Soon they overcame their timidity and were proud to let the Suggestion Department know their names when they had ideas to propose. One of Patterson's main purposes was to encourage his workers to think. To stimulate thought he caused placards bearing the word "Think" to be placed on all the factory walls. How well his admonition was heeded was shown in the hundreds of suggestions that began to flow in.

The Suggestion Department was started in 1894 when $30 was offered as first prize. In 1944, on the occasion of the fiftieth anniversary of the birth of the system, held under the auspices of the Labor-Management Committee thousands of dollars in War Bonds and Stamps was distributed in prizes by the Company. The first prize—a $1500 War Bond—was won by an assembler for devising a method of cleaning ball bearings that insures perfect action by the bearings. It can be applied wherever ball bearings are used. This suggestion was typical of the kind that win prizes.

Each year an average of 3,000 suggestions are received. The Suggestion System is open to all employees, whether in the factory, office or in the selling field. A salesman in Des Moines received a prize for suggesting a new way to develop the individual need of a merchant for a special type of machine.

When workers realize that individual incentive is recognized and rewarded they pay more attention to tools, processes, and methods, all in the hope that they can improve themselves and be singled out for cash and commendation. The result is that the NCR has 22,000 eyes and ears on the job of seeking out corrections and improvements throughout the plant. Every bench and lathe becomes an observation post. The entire factory is suggestion-minded. Putting it another way, the thought engine of the factory is run by an 11,000 mind power and not by a mind power stoked by a few men at the top.

Achievement is not only recognized and rewarded but publicized. The factory publication prints the news and picture of workers who win prizes. Thus all the employees become familiar with the faces and feats of their successful co-workers and are inspired to do likewise. They know that the tonic of opportunity is at everybody's elbow.

The pattern of NCR industrial relations has been defined by Allyn in this wise:

"Since money talks many industrialists still labor under the delusion that it is the only medium of communication with employees. The pay envelope, however, is only one link. There is likewise the human link if we are to forge the chain of complete management-employee understanding. You cannot put a heart throb into a machine but you can humanize the relations of the man at the machine.

"Management should speak to employees and employees should speak to management. What do employees want to hear that will establish a real kinship with management? First comes the desire to be kept informed of management policies and objectives. The reason is obvious. The worker's future and that of his family is bound up in the future of the Company. It is not idle curiosity that inspires this state of mind. It is dictated by the instinct of self preservation.

"Employees like to be told about factory changes

before they are made. Here you touch a basic human weakness. There is usually more mis-information than real information about most things. The average man, unhappily, is likely to grasp at the mis-information. Few agencies are more dangerous or disruptive in a plant than rumor. It makes for fear, apprehension, dissatisfaction, and finally disaffection. Hence it is wise to sterilize rumor before it starts and thus put the factory rumor-monger out of business. Nothing is ever lost by taking employees into your confidence.

"A third factor is the desire of employees to have the feel of identity with the organization. It helps to neutralize the impersonal phase of big industry and gives the lift of pride to performance no matter how humble it may be. Thus the worker is no longer the forgotten man—a cog in a large machine.

"One basic handicap in some industrial organizations is that they expand so fast that the individual worker is submerged. Factory team-work is gained but individual initiative is often lost. The size of a plant, however, need not stifle individual ambition as our experience shows.

"If management is to speak to employees it must have channels of communication. We have provided many. Someone has said that the middle name of the NCR is 'meetings.' We have meetings galore all to the end not only of bringing all our people together in groups or *en masse*, but of keeping them advised about what is going on. No conduit to the workers is more effective.

"Once a month, for example, or at the call of the executives, we have a foremen's meeting which is attended by all the Company's officers. Reports are made on phases of operation in the preceding month. Financial figures are revealed. In this way the foremen sit in with management and discuss the problems of the business. At these meetings division heads deal with their activities which may be Sales, Engineering, or Product Development. The foremen, and through them, the workers, get a comprehensive view of every phase of policy, production, and distribution. They are made to feel that they are 'in the know' which stimulates pride and ambition.

"The management-employee relation is as fluid and continuing as life itself. It is never concluded by the adoption of a resolution, the shaping of a policy, or the projection of a fresh idea. Management must be alert and alive to the changing pattern of labor and industry. Industry needs satisfied workers as much as satisfied customers. You can have them, as we have them, if you combine the elements of Head, Hand and Heart."

Fortifying NCR management is the varied experience and qualifications of the Board of Directors which embodies a balance between the Company and outside business and finance. As Chairman of the Board Colonel Deeds brings to the post his

seasoned knowledge of human and industrial needs
and direction so indispensable to the shaping of
policy. Allyn's long and intimate contact with
practically every phase of the business is an invaluable asset. Kindl, as head of production and Wilson
as chief of sales, lend technical authority to Board
decisions. Kettering's scientific achievements, his
success as industrialist, and his early connection with
the Company make a significant contribution to the
group.

Gordon S. Rentschler's membership on the Board
has a peculiar interest. The first casting made by
him as an apprentice in his father's business, the
Sohn and Rentschler Foundry at Hamilton, Ohio,
was for a National cash register. Today, as Chairman of the Board of the National City Bank of New
York City, he has at his command the facilities of
the greatest international financial institution in the
country. Thus he can evaluate NCR operations in
any part of the globe. Charles S. McCain is a leading figure in the financial world with a broad background and a notable record as constructive financial
counsellor. He was President of the Bankers Trust
Company of Little Rock, Arkansas, and later President of the Chase National Bank of New York City.
Sherman Peer, a director in the Allen-Wales subsidiary, is a prominent lawyer and conspicuous
citizen of Ithaca, New York. He is Vice President
and director of the Tompkins County Trust Company and President of the Cornell University Re-

search Foundation. An outstanding figure in the savings bank domain, Walter H. Bennett is a Trustee of the Emigrant Industrial Savings Bank of New York City. He entered banking by way of the retail dry goods field and served with R. G. Dun and Company. As President of the Winters National Bank and Trust Company, Walter H. J. Behm is Dayton's foremost banker. Eminent among her civic-minded citizens he is a link with larger community affairs. Here then, is a group of men who, out of highest authority and rich experience, are qualified to shape Company course.

Realizing that the men charged with the training of new workers as well as the training of older employees on new jobs, will play an important part in peacetime production the Company financed a Job Relations Course for all supervisors, foremen, and job foremen. It was part of the Training Within Industry program sponsored by the War Manpower Commission. The connecting link between the supervisor and the men under him is job relations. Hence the importance of a complete comprehension of it.

The course was held in Chicago for three reasons. One was as a reward for the good work done by supervisors, foremen, and job foremen on the war production program. The second was that by getting the men away from their work and the factory environment they could concentrate on the classes without interruption. Third was that inclusion of many new foremen who had risen from the ranks marked them as part of management.

The Company sent 334 supervisors, foremen, and job foremen to Chicago in four groups between February 14 and May 1, 1944. The classes were held in the assembly rooms of the Chicago office and were under the direction of R. E. Kline, head of the NCR Educational Department and J. N. Garwood, a supervisor. The course emphasized four bases for good job relations. They were: "Let Each Worker Know How He is Getting Along," "Give Credit When Due," "Tell People In Advance About Changes," and "Make The Most Of Every Worker's Ability." During the course actual instances were brought before the various groups and analyzed according to the method taught to meet the situations. After the return to Dayton two more class periods were held to complete ten additional hours of training. Upon completion each man was certified that he had completed the Training Within Industry Job Relations Course.

The sessions were addressed by Colonel Deeds, Allyn, and other executives. On the theory that what is good for salesmen is also good for foremen, the members of the Chicago NCR selling force had a part in the meetings. The factory men got a closeup of the way the product of their hands is sold. They were also shown installations of NCR machines in three large Chicago department stores. This was part of the NCR policy that workers should know about all phases of the business.

Pleasure mixed with study at Chicago. Every man was provided with a booklet telling what to see in the city. He was also furnished with pocket money for incidental expenses. Every one returned to Dayton with his educational outlook broadened and a deeper understanding of what his job meant.

An effective link with personnel is the Horseshoe Room which has developed into an institution known from coast to coast. Originally the executives, numbering not more than twenty, lunched in the Officers Club. Today two hundred men lunch at a table shaped like a horseshoe. They include executives, supervisors, department heads, and foremen. The shape of the table permits informal companionship. Frequently distinguished guests speak to the group. The Horseshoe Room is therefore not only a forum of useful information but a sounding board for the entire factory.

The NCR Labor-Management Committee, recruited equally from management and labor, is a further link with personnel. Here management talks with men and men talk with management. At each monthly meeting a definite subject such as Care of Tools, Cutting Waste, Bottlenecks, Safety, Absenteeism, or Fire Protection is discussed. Usually a playlet is presented by a cast drawn from management and labor to dramatize the subject of the meeting. The Labor-Management Committee has its own publication which goes to every worker, thus giving wide publicity to the team work that exists between the executive and worker levels.

When the Second World War broke this team work paid high dividends in loyalty and service. The NCR War Production Drive Organization, with an equal representation of management and labor, was set up. The chairman of the Planning Committee was J. N. Garwood, acting for management, while the co-chairman was Lloyd E. Bell, a worker in the screw-making department who represented labor and the NCR Employees Independent Union. This Committee was supervised by an Advisory Committee made up of executives of the company and officers of the Union. Various other committees dealt with every phase of production from care of tools to the prevention of breakdowns.

On the occasion of the presentation of the first Navy "E" pennant to the NCR—it received five "E" pennants in all for its war production—the following pledge was made by all the factory workers:

"We, the more than 9,000 Americans constituting the forces of the National Cash Register Company at Dayton, make this pledge:

"The resources of this organization, the skill and experience of its people, their loyalty and their willingness to sacrifice, are ready for any call that may be made by our Government.

"The integrity of loyal workmanship and the determination to win this war, will go into every piece of war material that leaves this plant. Wherever it may go, whatever it may be designed to do, we pledge you that it will be an 'E' product, made by 'E' men and women."

In that usually sensitive industrial situation which is labor relations the NCR has set a standard. Years ago an Advisory Board, then an Employees Council and later a House of Representatives, which was elected by ballot of the workers, dealt with all labor matters to be taken up with the management. On September 13, 1938 the NCR Employees Independent Union was organized which has functioned ever since.

The President of the Union is W. H. Creamer, Sr., who rose from news boy to the leadership of the factory workers. When I asked him to define labor policy at the factory he said:

"Here at the NCR we do not bargain over labor matters because bargaining implies distrust. We discuss things."

Every one who has ever sought a position in an industrial, and for that matter any other kind of corporation, remembers the cross-examination to which he was subjected when he applied. To oral queries is added a questionnaire. The President of the NCR believes that this procedure should be a fifty-fifty proposition, since the employment sought may become a life work. In other words, the applicant should have the right to ask a few questions himself. As the President sees it he should get answers to these queries: Does the company have a popular product for which there is constant need and demand? Are research and engineering adequate? What are employee relations? Can the company earn a profit? Does it follow conservative financial policies?

The employee relations established by NCR have developed a continuity of service that stands out in any appraisal of the Company. I have already referred to the Twenty-five Year Club with its 1,461 members. Into the record of the club are woven stimulating and inspiring stories of men who have risen from the ranks to high position.

The careers of Colonel Deeds, S. C. Allyn and Vice-Presidents Carl Kindl, John M. Wilson and George A. Marshall have been recounted. In 1908 Harry M. Williams started in as chemist in the testing department at $16 a week. Today he is Vice-President in charge of Engineering and Research. Two years after Williams went on the payroll G. R. Lohnes began as clerk in the Treasurer's office. Now he is Treasurer of the Company. The late J. H. Barringer's first job was as tracer in the wood cabinet department. When he retired he was First Vice President and General Manager. Another conspicuous rise has been that of Dr. F. G. Barr, Vice-President and head of Industrial Relations. He started as assistant in the Hygiene Department. Carl W. Beust's first pay was $6 a week as messenger and office boy in the Patent Department. He is now Head of the Patent Department. J. K. Owen's initial task was to order printing for the Advertising Manager. Now he sits in the Advertising Manager's chair. Earl E. Storms began service with the Company as an inspector. He is now Factory Manager. William E. Bahl has gone from errand boy to Assistant Factory Managership. Beginning as file clerk Robert S. Oelman has advanced to be Assistant Vice President. Eliseo C. Miro was first employed as English-Spanish stenographer in the main office of the Spanish subsidiary. In 1943 he was named Overseas Sales Method Director. Two other one time stenograhers, L. M. Guelich and H. D. Hussey, are Office Supervisor and Purchasing Agent respectively. Edward Grabeman has risen from dish-washer to be Chief of the Commissary. Herbert E. Paul began as assembler at 13 cents an hour and is now Inspection Division Manager. Another former assembler, J. N. Garwood, is a supervisor and a member of many of the most important management-labor committees in the factory.

The Sales Department has also registered an impressive roster of promotions from the ranks. L. S. McCallister's first position with the Company was as $12 a week clerk in the Wilmington office. To-day he is Assistant Sales Manager. Beginning as office man in Manchester, New Hampshire, Roger W. Burman served as Manager for Europe and of the Company in Japan and is at present Branch Manager in New York City. Another ex-office man, Howard

S. Whiffen, is head of the North-Eastern Division, while still another, Leo Stahl, is manager of the Central Division. Carl W. Hauser's rise is typical of what NCR men have accomplished. He began as porter in the Detroit office. Now he is manager of the Pacific Division.

You have travelled a long way through these pages from the day when James Ritty stood before the automatic mechanism that recorded the revolutions of a ship's propeller and conceived the idea for the cash register. You have witnessed the birth of an industry and watched it develop into worldwide dimensions, impressing its need and service wherever men trade and money is handled. For six decades the influence of one man has been manifest in practically every aspect of this far-reaching expansion, from the humanizing of production to the distribution of output. If, as Emerson wrote, "an institution is the lengthened shadow of a man," then The National Cash Register Company is the lengthened shadow of John H. Patterson.

THE END

INDEX

TECHNOLOGY AND SOCIETY

An Arno Press Collection

Ardrey, R[obert] L. **American Agricultural Implements.** In two parts. 1894

Arnold, Horace Lucien and Fay Leone Faurote. **Ford Methods and the Ford Shops.** 1915

Baron, Stanley [Wade]. **Brewed in America:** A History of Beer and Ale in the United States. 1962

Bathe, Greville and Dorothy. **Oliver Evans:** A Chronicle of Early American Engineering. 1935

Bendure, Zelma and Gladys Pfeiffer. **America's Fabrics:** Origin and History, Manufacture, Characteristics and Uses. 1946

Bichowsky, F. Russell. **Industrial Research.** 1942

Bigelow, Jacob. **The Useful Arts:** Considered in Connexion with the Applications of Science. 1840. Two volumes in one

Birkmire, William H. **Skeleton Construction in Buildings.** 1894

Boyd, T[homas] A[lvin]. **Professional Amateur:** The Biography of Charles Franklin Kettering. 1957

Bright, Arthur A[aron], Jr. **The Electric-Lamp Industry:** Technological Change and Economic Development from 1800 to 1947. 1949

Bruce, Alfred and Harold Sandbank. **The History of Prefabrication.** 1943

Carr, Charles C[arl]. **Alcoa, An American Enterprise.** 1952

Cooley, Mortimer E. **Scientific Blacksmith.** 1947

Davis, Charles Thomas. **The Manufacture of Paper.** 1886

Deane, Samuel. **The New-England Farmer,** or Georgical Dictionary. 1822

Dyer, Henry. **The Evolution of Industry.** 1895

Epstein, Ralph C. **The Automobile Industry:** Its Economic and Commercial Development. 1928

Ericsson, Henry. **Sixty Years a Builder:** The Autobiography of Henry Ericsson. 1942

Evans, Oliver. **The Young Mill-Wright and Miller's Guide.** 1850

Ewbank, Thomas. **A Descriptive and Historical Account of Hydraulic and Other Machines for Raising Water,** Ancient and Modern. 1842

Field, Henry M. **The Story of the Atlantic Telegraph.** 1893

Fleming, A. P. M. **Industrial Research in the United States of America.** 1917

Van Gelder, Arthur Pine and Hugo Schlatter. **History of the Explosives Industry in America.** 1927

Hall, Courtney Robert. **History of American Industrial Science.** 1954

Hungerford, Edward. **The Story of Public Utilities.** 1928

Hungerford, Edward. **The Story of the Baltimore and Ohio Railroad, 1827-1927.** 1928

Husband, Joseph. **The Story of the Pullman Car.** 1917

Ingels, Margaret. **Willis Haviland Carrier, Father of Air Conditioning.** 1952

Kingsbury, J[ohn] E. **The Telephone and Telephone Exchanges:** Their Invention and Development. 1915

Labatut, Jean and Wheaton J. Lane, eds. **Highways in Our National Life:** A Symposium. 1950

Lathrop, William G[ilbert]. **The Brass Industry in the United States.** 1926

Lesley, Robert W., John B. Lober and George S. Bartlett. **History of the Portland Cement Industry in the United States.** 1924

Marcosson, Isaac F. **Wherever Men Trade:** The Romance of the Cash Register. 1945

Miles, Henry A[dolphus]. **Lowell, As It Was, and As It Is.** 1845

Morison, George S. **The New Epoch:** As Developed by the Manufacture of Power. 1903

Olmsted, Denison. **Memoir of Eli Whitney, Esq.** 1846

Passer, Harold C. **The Electrical Manufacturers, 1875-1900.** 1953

Prescott, George B[artlett]. **Bell's Electric Speaking Telephone.** 1884

Prout, Henry G. **A Life of George Westinghouse.** 1921

Randall, Frank A. **History of the Development of Building Construction in Chicago.** 1949

Riley, John J. **A History of the American Soft Drink Industry:** Bottled Carbonated Beverages, 1807-1957. 1958

Salem, F[rederick] W[illiam]. **Beer, Its History and Its Economic Value as a National Beverage.** 1880

Smith, Edgar F. **Chemistry in America.** 1914

Steinman, D[avid] B[arnard]. **The Builders of the Bridge:** The Story of John Roebling and His Son. 1950

Taylor, F[rank] Sherwood. **A History of Industrial Chemistry.** 1957

Technological Trends and National Policy, Including the Social Implications of New Inventions. Report of the Subcommittee on Technology to the National Resources Committee. 1937

Thompson, John S. **History of Composing Machines.** 1904

Thompson, Robert Luther. **Wiring a Continent:** The History of the Telegraph Industry in the United States, 1832-1866. 1947

Tilley, Nannie May. **The Bright-Tobacco Industry, 1860-1929.** 1948

Tooker, Elva. **Nathan Trotter:** Philadelphia Merchant, 1787-1853. 1955

Turck, J. A. V. **Origin of Modern Calculating Machines.** 1921

Tyler, David Budlong. **Steam Conquers the Atlantic.** 1939

Wheeler, Gervase. **Homes for the People,** In Suburb and Country. 1855